Words Their Way

Words and Strategies for Academic Success

VOLUME II

Glenview, Illinois • Boston, Massachusetts • Chandler, Arizona • Hoboken, New Jersey

ISBN-13: 978-1-4284-3984-9
ISBN-10:   1-4284-3984-6

1   16

ALWAYS LEARNING

PEARSON

Words Their Way
Words and Strategies for Academic Success

I wanted to impress this new student in our class. But each time I tried to say something, I couldn't think of the right word to use.

When I was talking to my older cousin, he used some words I never heard before. I was too embarassed to tell him I didn't understand what he was talking about.

I didn't do well on my test. There were just too many words on it that I didn't know.

Sometimes when I'm reading, I come across words I don't know. That makes it hard to understand what's going on.

Writing is a problem too. My teacher said one way I can improve is to pay attention to the vocabulary in my writing.

Words of Advice

• Learn words. And when you learn them, learn how they work.

• Words have roots; learn to recognize the roots and what they mean.

• Learn vocabulary strategies, such as using context clues and consulting reference materials. These strategies will help you determine the meanings of words.

• Learn the vocabulary of your subject-area classes (Math, Science, Social Studies) and the words that you use in school in general.

Vocabulary is like a tree. It begins with the roots and then just grows and grows.

Contents

Contents

Contents

Contents

LIST 1   cred

accredit
credentials
credible
credit
incredulous

Cred is a Latin root that means "believe."

- Words containing *cred* usually have something to do with believing, having faith in, or trusting.
- Use *cred* as a clue to meaning when you come across words that contain this root.

When you see *cred,* think of *incredible* ("not believable").

Clues to Meaning Use *cred* as a clue to the meanings of the underlined words.

- The principal <u>accredited</u>, or authorized, vice-principal Ms. Ojekwu to represent him at the meeting. Her <u>credentials</u>, such as her education and references, are very impressive.

- We were <u>incredulous</u> after Cameron told that unbelievable story. No one liked that he made up that story to hide a mistake, and we gave him no <u>credit</u> for finally being honest with us. It will be hard to think of him as <u>credible</u> in the future.

LIST 2   gno

agnostic
prognosis
prognosticate

Gno is a Greek root that means "to know."

- Words containing *gno* usually have something to do with knowing or learning.

When you see *gno,* think of *diagnose* (to learn or come "to know" by examination or tests).

Clues to Meaning Use *gno* as a clue to the meanings of the underlined words.

Aisha Doctor, what <u>prognosis</u> can you give that will tell me what to expect as the disease progresses?

Dr. Jones It's hard to say exactly. In order to <u>prognosticate</u>, or forecast what is likely to happen in your case, I will use new software that is platform <u>agnostic</u>. It can run on any computer operating system, such as Windows or Mac OS X.

Aisha Perhaps I can use the software on my computer at home to learn about the disease.

Cogn is a Latin root that means "to know."

- Words containing *cogn* usually have something to do with knowing.
- When you see *cogn,* think of *re**cogn**ize* (realize that something or someone has been "known" before).

Clues to Meaning Use *cogn* as a clue to the meanings of the underlined words.

The spy was <u>incognito</u> because she did not want to be known, or recognized. She was following an enemy agent who had been arrested on a minor charge, but he was released on his own <u>recognizance</u> when he agreed to appear in court. The spy thought that the enemy agent might be aware that he was being tailed. She would certainly be <u>cognizant</u> of a tail if their roles were reversed. The spy's <u>cognition</u> of this possibility made her aware of the need to be cautious.

• •

In Your Notebook Write each word, its root, and its meaning.

Synonyms and Antonyms as Context Clues

You can use context clues to understand words you do not know. Some context clues are synonyms or antonyms—words that mean the same or the opposite of a word.

Mark said Leo's excuse was <u>*credible*</u>*. I agreed that it was* <u>*believable*</u>*.*

In these sentences, the context clues show you that *believable* and *credible* are synonyms—they have similar meanings. The word *believable* helps you understand that *credible* means "convincing."

The following sentence uses an antonym for a context clue:

Mark said Leo's excuse was <u>*incredible*</u>*,* <u>*but*</u> *I thought it was* <u>*believable*</u>*.*

The prefix *in* can mean "not" or "the opposite of." The word *incredible* means "not believable." The conjunction *but* is a context clue that a contrast, and maybe an antonym, will follow.

Apply and Extend

Have you heard these expressions?
- give credit where credit is due
- buy something on credit

What is believed in each case?

▪ List 1

Write a synonym, or word with a similar meaning, for each list word. For example, one synonym for *credible* is *reliable*.

▪ List 2

Find one more word with the Greek root *gno*. Write a sentence using your new word and one or two list words. Provide context that shows that you understand the meanings of the words.

▪ List 3

Write a sentence that shows the meaning of each word. For example, the word *cognition* means "the process of knowing" or "awareness": *He has cognition that sometimes his actions are foolish.*

Clue Review Play a word game with one of your classmates. Choose one of the list words. Give your partner a clue about the word. Did your partner guess the word correctly? If not, provide another clue until your partner correctly identifies the word. Then switch roles.

brawny
burly
dominant
durable
magnitude
massive
sturdy
vigorous

Use Context as Clues to Meaning

Precise words can help readers picture the unique features and qualities of people, places, and things in stories.

Read these sentences. Which one helps you understand the ambassador better?

> The ambassador knew her assignment was important.

> As the ambassador presented her **credentials** to the embassy guard, she suddenly realized the **magnitude** of her assignment.

The second sentence is stronger. The precise word *magnitude* suggests the great significance of the assignment. The word *credentials* has the root *cred,* which means "believe." *Credentials* give credibility, or believability, to the official power granted to the ambassador. *Magnitude* and *credentials* show that the ambassador's job is very important, and it gives her power.

Read the following story. How does the context help you understand the meanings of the underlined words?

> All three hikers were big and <u>burly</u>, but Mo, who worked out at the gym every day, had the most powerful muscles and was the <u>brawniest</u>. He also had a <u>dominant</u> personality and liked to be in charge. His friends Andy and Easton usually went along with what Mo wanted to do—and what Mo wanted to do was climb a local mountain.

> As the three approached the mountain, they were amazed by its <u>magnitude</u>. It was much larger than they had expected.

> "I know you are worried," Mo said to his friends, "but we can do this. We are all healthy and <u>sturdy</u> enough to get to the top."

> The three men then moved to the nearest path and, full of energy, started walking at a <u>vigorous</u> pace. Soon they came upon their first obstacle, a <u>massive</u> boulder. It was bulky and heavy, but they worked together and were able to move it. The men then moved on. In a short time the path became steep and rocky. They were glad that they were wearing such <u>durable</u> boots that could withstand the conditions.

> When they reached the top, they were tired from the exercise. "We did it," said Easton, "but now we'll have to climb down."

In Your Notebook Write the list words. Next to each word, write another word that you associate with it. For example, for *sturdy,* you might write *strong.*

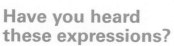

Have you heard these expressions?

- durable goods
- dominant gene

Context Clues

Authors sometimes embed a word or phrase in their writing that helps you figure out the meaning of an unfamiliar word. That word or phrase may be a direct definition or an explanation set off by punctuation, such as a pair of commas, parentheses, or dashes, or by a single comma or dash if the explanatory word or phrase is at the beginning or end of the sentence. See how the punctuation in these sentences sets off the definitions of the underlined words.

> The <u>ambassador</u> (the official representative of our country) was sent overseas to make peace. This was a <u>precarious</u>, or dangerous and uncertain, assignment. If she failed, the result would be national <u>ignominy</u>—shame and dishonor.

When you come across an unknown word, see if the punctuation marks set off a clue to its meaning.

Apply and Extend

■ Think about a task you have done that required strength. Which of the list words would you use to describe the strength you needed? Remember that strength can be mental, such as a *massive* effort needed to earn an A in a class.

■ Choose one of the list words. Use a thesaurus to find a synonym for the word. Then write a sentence using the word and its synonym to show the meaning in context.

Word History Choose an interesting word from this week's lesson. What can you find out about the history and origins of your word? Answer the following questions:

- From which language did your word derive?

- What is the first recorded instance of its use in English?

- What is one interesting fact you learned about the word?

- List related words that you find.

prim, princ | LIST 1

Prim is a Latin root that means "first." Another way to spell this prefix is *princ*.

- Words containing *prim* or *princ* usually have something to do with being first, chief, or highest. When you see *prim* or *princ*, think of **prim**ary ("first" in time, order, or importance).

LIST 1

primate
primeval
primitive
principality
principle

Clues to Meaning Use *prim* and *princ* as clues to the meanings of the underlined words.

- Humans, apes, and monkeys belong to the highest order of mammals, called <u>primates</u>.

- Many of the ancient trees in the <u>primeval</u> forest of Muir Woods National Monument, near San Francisco, California, are more than 600 years old.

- Scientists believe that Yellowstone National Park's famous geyser, Old Faithful, may be home to a <u>primitive</u> life form—a very, very early kind—that thrives in hot springs.

- Prince Albert II is the ruler of Monaco, a tiny <u>principality</u> on the French Riviera.

- The Declaration of Independence sets forth the basic <u>principles</u> of American democracy: those most important beliefs of freedom, equality, and the rights of individuals.

sequ, sec | LIST 2

Sequ is a Latin root that means "follow." Another way to spell this root is *sec*.

- Words containing *sequ* or *sec* usually have something to do with following.
- Use *sequ* and *sec* as clues to meaning when you come across words that contain this root. When you see *sequ* or *sec*, think of **sequ**ence (the "following" of one thing after another).

LIST 2

consecutive
obsequious
persecute
secondary
sect
sequester
subsequently

Clues to Meaning Use *sequ* and *sec* as clues to the meanings of the underlined words.

- After performing in <u>consecutive</u> concerts every day for a week, Ramon was exhausted. He wanted to <u>sequester</u> himself in his dressing room so he could rest. Before he could do so, however, an <u>obsequious</u> fan found him in the hallway. It was hard to be rude to such a follower when she wouldn't stop praising his music.

- In the first book of that series, Mia and Nate both feel as if their parents <u>persecute</u> them, punishing them for the smallest misdeed. In the story's sequel, the two young people plan to leave home and join a <u>sect</u>, a group of people who follow the same beliefs and principles.

- Although his first plan was to bunt, Keagan <u>subsequently</u> hit the ball out of the park. He decided that from now on, his <u>secondary</u> plan would always be to hit the ball as hard as he could.

· ·

In Your Notebook Write the list words. Next to each word, write its meaning. Then write the context clues from the context sentence that helped you figure out its meaning.

Context Clues

Sometimes surrounding phrases or sentences will help you to understand an unknown word by restating or reinforcing its meaning.

> Shar attends cooking school for three <u>consecutive</u> days every <u>Monday, Tuesday, and Wednesday</u>.

In this sentence, the context clue—the list of days—gives you a hint about what *consecutive* might mean by restating or reinforcing it. When this kind of context clue is present, it could be helpful to substitute the phrase or word for the word you don't know:

> Shar attends cooking school every Monday, Tuesday, and Wednesday.

When you are unsure of a word's meaning, look at the text around it for clues to meaning.

Apply and Extend

■ List 1

Write one sentence using as many of the list words as you can. Challenge yourself. Can you use all five words in one sentence?

■ List 1

Think about how the words *primate, primeval,* and *primitive* are related in meaning. Can a primate be primeval? Can a primate be primitive? Write a sentence or two using these three words.

■ List 2

The word *sequester* has more than one meaning. Look up the word in a dictionary. Then use the word in a sentence for each of the meanings listed. Use context that shows you understand the different meanings.

Rap It Up Working with a classmate, choose a word from the week's lesson. Use the word and its meaning to create a short poem or rap such as the one below. Compile your rap with other classmates' raps into a Rap It Up notebook.

> Primary, secondary, tertiary, more—
> Trying to think sequentially
> will drive me out the door!

Did you know?
Principle and *principal* both contain the root *princ,* but their meanings are very different. A *principle* is a noun meaning "a fundamental truth." *Principal* can be an adjective ("most important") or a noun ("head of a school").

LIST WORDS

act
balcony
dramatic
monologue
scene
solo
stage directions
staging

Use Context as Clues to Meaning

The Italian phrase *prima donna* translates as "first lady" and refers to the principal female singer in an opera. The Latin root *prim* means "first," and *donna* comes from the Latin word for "lady," *domina*. Over the years, *prima donna* has also come to mean a temperamental person.

In theater, a prima donna may recite a speech called a *monologue*. The word *monologue* has the Greek roots *mono* and *logue*.

mono (one) + logue (speech) = monologue (a long speech by one person)

At the left are more words related to performing and the theater. You may come across these words in your language arts studies.

Read the following dialogue. How does the context help you understand the meanings of the underlined words?

Antoine I'm so nervous about this play! I just know I'll forget my <u>monologue</u>. My legs start shaking when I start speaking alone on the stage, and I forget my <u>stage directions</u>. Am I supposed to exit left or right after my scene?

Adrienne Try not to be so <u>dramatic</u>! You'll be fine. The play is short; it has only two major parts, and each of the two <u>acts</u> has three <u>scenes</u>. Your fellow actors will help you, and the <u>staging</u> is great, with fabulous sets and costumes. This play is going to be awesome—and even more so because I get to sing by myself on stage. Now I have to go get ready for my <u>solo</u>!

Antoine Promise me that when I'm on stage, you'll be in the <u>balcony</u>, where the seats overlook the stage, looking down at me and smiling!

Adrienne You bet. Front row.

• •

In Your Notebook Write each list word. Then combine each word with an adjective or noun to create a short, descriptive phrase. Examples are *short acts* or *soprano solo*. Make sure the context shows your understanding of each list word.

Using a Dictionary

What could you do if the context of the word *solo* had not helped you figure out its meaning? You could consult a dictionary. A dictionary is an invaluable reference source. Whenever you want to learn about words, start with a dictionary. It contains thousands of words, which are listed in alphabetical order. Each word has an entry that provides information about the word: spelling, pronunciation, definition or definitions, usage, and history. A dictionary can be a printed book or online.

Consult a dictionary when you want to

- find the pronunciation of a word
- verify a word's meaning
- determine a word's precise meaning
- clarify a word's part of speech
- learn about a word's etymology

Have you heard these expressions?
- a hard act to follow
- to steal the scene
- drama queen

Apply and Extend

Actors in a play can speak to each other, address the audience, or even talk to themselves in words, verse, or song. Write two or three sentences about the similarities and differences among a *monologue, dialogue,* and *solo.* To check meaning, use a dictionary.

Draw a sketch of a stage for plays that illustrates as many of the list words as you can. Write a label for each list word you put into the drawing.

Skit With a partner, add stage directions to the scene between Adrienne and Antoine. Give the characters gestures, props, and movements around the stage. Then act out the skit for the class.

LESSON 5

Word Parts and Meanings
pat, mat, frat

LIST 1

pat

expatriate
patriotic
patron
patronize

Pat is a Latin root that means "father."

- Words containing *pat* usually have something to do with fatherhood.
- When you see *pat,* think of **paternal** (of or like a "father"; fatherly).

Clues to Meaning Use *pat* as a clue to the meanings of the underlined words.

- The government decided to <u>expatriate</u> all of those people who had participated in the attempted revolution and gave them one week to leave the country.

- Some people consider it <u>patriotic</u> to criticize their country, because pointing out its faults shows they love and are loyal to their country.

- As a <u>patron</u> of the theater, I try to support actors and playwrights with money, help, and attendance at plays.

- To support our community businesses, we <u>patronize</u> only local stores instead of shopping at malls or big chain stores.

LIST 2

mat

maternal
matriarch
matrimony
matrix

Mat is a Latin root that means "mother."

- Words containing *mat* usually have something to do with motherhood.
- When you see *mat,* think of **maternity** ("motherhood").

Clues to Meaning Use *mat* as a clue to the meanings of the underlined words.

Fifty years ago my grandmother and grandfather entered into <u>matrimony</u>, and they remained married until my grandfather's death two years ago. Their marriage was the <u>matrix</u> of our family, the relationship where our family began. They had five children, and my grandmother always had strong <u>maternal</u> feelings for all of them. After my grandfather's death, my grandmother became our <u>matriarch</u>, the head of the family, until her own death earlier this year. We miss her every day.

18

fraternal
fraternization
fraternize
interfraternity

Frat is a Latin root that means "brother."

- Words containing the root *frat* usually have something to do with brothers or a relationship such as brothers might have.
- Use *frat* as a clue to meaning when you come across words that contain this root.

- When you see *frat,* think of **fraternity** (college young men getting together like "brothers").

Clues to Meaning Use *frat* as a clue to the meanings of the underlined words.

- My uncle belongs to a <u>fraternal</u> organization. He goes to meetings and hangs out with his buddies every Friday night.

- During the Allied occupation of Nazi Germany, <u>fraternization</u> between American soldiers and German civilians was strictly forbidden—there was to be no social interaction.

- When the competition was finally over, the two basketball teams were able to <u>fraternize</u> freely, shooting baskets and building friendships.

- In a show of <u>interfraternity</u> cooperation, the men's social organizations on campus decided to work together to donate their time and effort at the local food pantry.

• •

In Your Notebook Write each list word and its meaning. Next to each word, write a synonym. To check a meaning, use a dictionary.

Etymology Study

Etymology is the "explanation of the origin and history of a word." When you see word parts whose etymology you know, you can figure out what the word means. For example, the word *expatriate* has two Latin origins, *ex* meaning "out of" and *patria* meaning "fatherland," or native country. Knowing that, you can deduce that to expatriate someone (verb) is to send the person out of the person's own country. An expatriate (noun) is a person who lives outside of his or her native country, whether or not by that person's choice.

■ List 1

Find one more word with the root *pat*. Write a sentence using your new word and one or two list words. Provide context that shows that you understand the meanings of the words.

■ List 2

Choose two words from the list and write a sentence using both. Provide context that shows you understand the meanings of both words.

■ List 3

Write a sentence or two explaining how students can fraternize with each other and help their community at the same time.

Act It Out Put your acting talent to work. Work with several classmates to perform a skit based on some of the passages in this lesson. Choose a narrator and students to play the characters in the passage. Become your character!

Did you know?

The Latin root for *sister* is *soror*. Similar roots are found in Sanskrit and Old Norse. Two English words with this root are *sorority* and *sororal*.

carbohydrate
exercise
mineral
prescription
protein
ration
virus
vitamin

Use Context as Clues to Meaning

You have already learned one meaning of the word *matrix*. In biology, *matrix* refers to the material between cells in the human body. What does it have to do with *mater* for "mother"? This material originated in the womb!

Our bodies depend on many elements to stay healthy. One of those is carbohydrates. The word *carbohydrate* has three parts. *Carbo* (like the word *carbon*) comes from the Latin word for coal, *carbonem*. *Hydr* (like the word *hydrogen*) comes from the Greek word for water, *hydor*. The suffix *ate* is used to name a compound.

**carbo (coal) + hydr (water) + ate (compound) = carbohydrate
(a compound that contains carbon and hydrogen)**

At the right are more words related to health and nutrition. You may come across these words in your health or science class.

Read the paragraph below. How does the context help you understand the meanings of the underlined words?

If you are looking for ways to be healthy, there are some simple changes you can make in your life. First, get moving! Get lots of aerobic <u>exercise</u>, such as biking, swimming, or jogging. Second, eat a balanced diet. Don't eat too many <u>carbohydrates</u>, such as rice, pasta, and bread. Instead, eat lean meat, fish, eggs, legumes, or dairy products. These will provide you with amino acids, which your body needs to make <u>proteins</u>. It is also important to get enough <u>vitamins</u> and <u>minerals</u>. Both are substances required to nourish the body. For example, eat citrus fruits—such as oranges—to get vitamin C, and drink milk for calcium. Third, to keep down your weight, watch how many calories you eat each day. Read the labels on food packages to find out the healthy <u>ration</u> of that food, the ideal amount to eat. Fourth, take only those medications that your doctor orders for you with a written <u>prescription</u>. And finally, if you do get a <u>virus</u>, such as a cold or the flu, stay in bed and drink plenty of fluids until you feel better.

• •

In Your Notebook Write each list word and its meaning. To check a meaning, use a dictionary.

Using a Glossary

A glossary is a specialized dictionary that covers a set of related words. Since different branches of the sciences and social studies have their own special vocabularies, books on those subjects usually have a glossary at the back of the book explaining words in that book and field of study. In addition to definitions, glossaries often provide the pronunciations and parts of speech for words. While a dictionary might give multiple definitions for a word, a glossary may offer only one or two definitions for the words, but they will be the definitions used in that field of study. The next time you are reading a science book or a social studies book, check the glossary to find the meanings of words you don't know.

The glossary at the back of this book includes the words presented in the lessons. You may want to consult it first when looking up your list words.

Have you heard these expressions?

- aerobic exercise
- animal, vegetable, or mineral?
- go viral
- vitamin-rich

Apply and Extend

■ Write two or three sentences that describe how you feel about exercise.

■ What do you do to stay healthy? Write two or three sentences, using some of the list words.

Clue Review Play a word game with one of your classmates. Choose one of the list words. Give your partner a clue about the word. Did your partner guess the word correctly? If not, provide another clue until your partner correctly identifies the word. Then switch roles.

urb

LIST 1

suburban
suburbanite
urbane
urbanization

Urb is a Latin root that means "city."
- Words containing *urb* usually have something to do with cities.
- When you see *urb,* think of **urb**an (having to do with "cities" or towns).

Clues to Meaning Use *urb* as a clue to the meanings of the underlined words.

- The growth of both population and industry in U.S. cities created a need for more buildings and better transportation, contributing to the process of <u>urbanization</u> in areas of the United States.

- Over time, the <u>suburban</u> lifestyle became popular with people who wanted to live near but not in a city.

- <u>Suburbanites</u>, those people who live in the suburbs, often commute to jobs in the cities.

- <u>Urbane</u> people who enjoy the finer things in life often find more cultural opportunities in cities.

agr

LIST 2

agrarian
agribusiness
agronomy

Agr is a Latin root that means "field."
- The word *agriculture* has two Latin roots.

    agr ("field") + colere ("tend"; "cultivate") = agriculture

    When you see *agr,* think of **agr**iculture (cultivating a "field"; producing crops and raising livestock).

Clues to Meaning Use *agr* as a clue to the meanings of the underlined words.

- In the early days of the United States, most people lived an <u>agrarian</u> lifestyle, supporting themselves by cultivating the soil and raising livestock.

- Today, students of <u>agronomy</u> are interested in applying their knowledge of crop production to a profession in <u>agribusiness</u>: the production, processing, and distribution of agricultural products.

LIST 3

semi

semicolon
semiconductor
semifinal
semimonthly
semiprofessional

Semi is a Latin prefix that means "half."

When you see *semi,* think of **semi**circle ("half" a circle).

Clues to Meaning Use *semi* as a clue to the meanings of the underlined words.

Marta Did you apply for the job at Rinehart Electronics, Jen? Working with <u>semiconductors</u> seemed like a good fit for you. They are certain kinds of minerals that conduct electricity better than an insulator but not as well as a metal. Since they are used to make transistors and integrated circuits, you would be great for the job.

Jen Well, I went for an interview, but the person who interviewed me criticized me for using a <u>semicolon</u> incorrectly on my résumé.

Marta It's important to use punctuation marks correctly; however, it's easy to forget some of the rules. When do you think you might hear about the job?

Jen This company only hires new employees <u>semimonthly</u>, or every two weeks, so if I do get hired, it won't be for two weeks.

Marta I know there may be a lot of people applying for the job, but I bet you'll at least get another interview.

Jen I hope so! In school, I was a <u>semiprofessional</u> athlete, so I got paid a bit for running in track. I made it to the <u>semifinals</u> but didn't get to the finals in one meet, so I know what it feels like to get that far in a competition. I really want to win this job!

In Your Notebook Write each list word and its meaning. What context clues helped you figure out word meaning? To check a meaning, use a dictionary.

Using a Thesaurus

If you need a synonym or antonym for a word such as *agrarian*, you can use a thesaurus. Some thesauruses are online; some are printed books. Most thesauruses are organized by category. To locate a particular word, look in the index at the back of the book, where words are organized alphabetically. The index will tell you where the entries are for the word's category or categories. In a thesaurus entry, you can expect to find information such as the word's part of speech, synonyms, and antonyms. Using a thesaurus can help you find precise, descriptive words to improve your writing.

Apply and Extend

▪ List 1

Write a question about one of the list words, showing that you understand the meaning of the word. Then show your question to a classmate to see if you have included enough context so that he or she can answer it.

▪ List 2

Write a brief dialogue using the list words, including context clues to show that you know the words' meanings.

▪ List 3

Several words in this lesson have the prefix *semi*. Find one more word with this prefix. Write a sentence using your new word and one or two list words. Provide context that shows that you understand the meanings of the words.

Did you know?

An urban legend is a made-up story that usually takes place in an urban setting. According to one urban legend, alligators live in the sewer system of New York City because people who had baby alligators as pets released them into the sewers when they grew and became dangerous.

Word Part Invention How much of a wordsmith are you? With a partner, combine word parts from this lesson with other letters or syllables to invent a new word. Then write a definition for the word based on the meanings of the word parts. Share the word and definition with classmates.

LIST WORDS

battalion
cavalry
dissenter
garrison
infantry
libel
stimulate
treason

Gather Meaning from Context

The word *antebellum* is actually a Latin word that has come into the English language. *Antebellum* has two parts: *ante* ("before") and *bellum* ("war"). In Latin, *antebellum* means "before the war." In English, at least in the United States, *antebellum* refers specifically to the period in the Deep South before the Civil War.

ante (before) + bellum (war) = antebellum (the period before the war)

At the left are words that describe various aspects of conflict. You may come across these words in your social studies class.

Read the following paragraphs. How does the context help you understand the meanings of the underlined words?

My great-great-grandfather, Robert Weber, was a lieutenant in Lieutenant Colonel Marshall C. Avery's <u>infantry</u> <u>battalion</u>, a large military unit of soldiers who fought on foot that had been sent to hold the line against the Union army in Tennessee. Colonel Avery decided to leave a <u>garrison</u> of twenty men to defend the town of Franklin. He promoted Lieutenant Weber to captain, left him in charge, and proceeded eastward toward the mountains with his four hundred or so remaining foot soldiers.

Captain Weber was happy with the assignment for two reasons. First, before the fighting began, whenever the topic of war with the North had come up, he had been a <u>dissenter</u>. He was a peaceful man and thought the country's differences could be solved without bloodshed. He had tried to <u>stimulate</u>, or promote, discussion around this possibility, but his friends had accused him of <u>treason</u> because they thought his actions betrayed their cause. One had written that in a letter to the local paper, which the editor had published. Weber had dismissed the accusation as nothing more than <u>libel</u>, or a lie about his character. He had no desire to kill anyone, but the idea of protecting civilians satisfied him greatly.

The other reason Captain Weber was happy with his new post was that it allowed him to perform his duties on horseback. His first act as commander was to select twenty soldiers from the battalion who could ride. He turned his garrison of infantrymen into a small <u>cavalry</u>.

• •

In Your Notebook Write a sentence for each list word, providing context that shows that you understand the meaning of each. To check a meaning, use a dictionary.

Word Story

The word *cavalry* comes from the Latin word *caballarius,* which means "horseman." Another English word that comes from *caballarius* is *cavalier,* a "mounted soldier" or "knight." The word *infantry* comes from the Latin word *infantem,* which means "youth" or "child" and is the source of the word *infant.* Behind these words is a story. In medieval Europe, more experienced soldiers or soldiers of higher social standing (especially knights) were more likely to fight on horseback. Younger, less experienced soldiers were more likely to fight on foot.

Apply and Extend

Did you know?
Squad, platoon, company, and *regiment* are terms that are used to describe military units.

▪ Use a print or online dictionary to identify the roots of the words *dissenter* and *stimulate.* Then explain the logical connection between the words' roots and their meanings.

▪ If a dissenter dissents, what is a person who commits treason called? Look in a dictionary or online to find this word, and then write one or two sentences with the word *treason* and your new word. Provide context to show that you understand the meaning of both.

Graphic Gallery Use your skills as a cartoonist to create a comic strip using words from this week's lesson. Draw pictures and write dialogue or use an online program to create the graphic text. How many of the words can you use? Compile the class's comic strips into a Graphic Gallery.

LIST 1

cide

herbicide
homicide
matricide
patricide

Cide is a Latin suffix that means "kill."

- Words containing *cide* usually have something to do with killing.
- Use *cide* as a clue to meaning when you come across words that contain this suffix.

When you see *cide*, think of *insecti**cide*** (a substance for "killing" insects).

Clues to Meaning Use *cide* as a clue to the meanings of the underlined words.

- Mr. Jackson used <u>herbicide</u> to destroy the weeds and then put up signs to warn people that he had sprayed the area with a poisonous chemical.

- Sylvia North was arrested on a <u>homicide</u> charge for killing her husband.

- Stories about murder have been told since ancient times. In Greek mythology, Orestes was guilty of <u>matricide</u> because he killed his mother, Clytemnestra. Oedipus committed <u>patricide</u> when he unknowingly killed his father.

LIST 2

cis

concise
excise
incision
precision

Cis is a Latin root that means "cut."

- Words containing *cis* usually have something to do with cutting.

When you see *cis,* think of *s**cis**sors* (a tool or instrument for "cutting").

Clues to Meaning Use *cis* as a clue to the meanings of the underlined words.

The doctor was <u>concise</u> as she briefly yet thoroughly explained the operation. During the surgery, she would make a cut, or <u>incision</u>, in Omar's abdomen. Then she would <u>excise</u> his appendix. The surgery would require <u>precision</u> and accuracy, but removing an appendix is a routine procedure.

Cap is a Latin root that means "head."

- Words containing *cap* usually have something to do with the head.
- When you see *cap,* think of **cap** (a hat for the "head").

Clues to Meaning Use *cap* as a clue to the meanings of the underlined words.

By 1787, members of the middle class of France had become increasingly wealthy. Despite their per capita wealth, or their wealth per person, these people had no power in the government. On July 14, 1789, members of the middle class attacked the Bastille, a prison in Paris, the capital city where the heads of government met. A captain, an army officer heading a group of the engineers in the French Army, composed a song that revolutionaries would sing as they marched into Paris in 1792. By the end of 1792, the revolutionaries put King Louis on trial for treason. He was found guilty, and on January 21, 1793, they used a machine called a guillotine to behead, or decapitate, him.

• •

In Your Notebook Write each list word and its meaning. Next to each word, write the context clues that helped you figure out the word's meaning. To check a meaning, use a dictionary.

Literary Allusions

A literary allusion is a reference to or a mention of a character, place, or event in literature. The reference is designed to call something to mind without mentioning it directly or explicitly. For example, an author might expect the reader to know about Greek mythological figures. An allusion to Oedipus suggests patricide, and a comparison of someone to Orestes hints at matricide.

Why might an author allude to the characters of Pinocchio, Peter Pan, or Cupid? Think about what each character is known for.

Apply and Extend

■ List 1

Several words in this lesson have the Latin suffix *cide.* What is the meaning of each? Another word with this suffix is *pesticide.* What do you think this word means? Make a list of other kinds of *-cides,* either real or made up, and explain what each one is.

■ List 2

Think about how *incision, precision,* and *concise* are related in meaning. Which word suggests accuracy? Which word suggests being brief? Write a sentence or two using these three words.

■ List 3

Write a question about one of the words that shows you understand its meaning, and write its answer. For example, for *capital* you could write *What is the capital of Texas? The Texas capital city is Austin.*

The Illustrated Word Sharpen your pencils—it's time to play a picture game. Divide a group into two teams. Write lesson words on cards and place them in a stack upside down. The first person on Team 1 takes a card, draws a picture that represents the word on the card, and shows the picture to his or her team. If team members guess the word in 30 seconds, the team gets a point. Now it's Team 2's turn.

Did you know?

Patricide comes from the Latin root *pater,* which means "father." It is related to *patriarch,* a father who is the ruler of a family or tribe, and *patriarchy,* an organization of which the father is head.

LIST WORDS

compass
concave
cone
convex
prism
radius
ratio
surface area

Gather Meaning from Context

A compass is an instrument for making precise measurements. A ship captain might use a compass to navigate, while a surveyor, a person who examines and measures land, might use a compass to measure distances.

The word *compass* comes from the Latin *com* and *passus.*

com (with) + passus (step) = compass

At the right are more words related to measurements, angles, and shapes. You may come across these words in your mathematics class.

Read the following sentences about mathematics. How does the context help you understand the meanings of the underlined words?

- The surveyor placed an orange traffic <u>cone</u> with a round base and pointed top next to his truck in the road. Then he used a <u>compass</u> to measure distances between points in the plot of land.

- "Hey, Mackenzie," said Ross, "when I shine light through this glass, I see different colors—red, yellow, blue, and more." Mackenzie replied, "You'll see orange, green, indigo, and violet, too. This is a <u>prism</u>. It was cut so that its ends are triangular. When light goes through it, the rays come apart, and you see all the colors of the spectrum. Its <u>surface area</u> is an amazing 81 inches. That is the sum of all the areas of the shapes on the outside."

- Henry said to Max, "I think of a cave because <u>concave</u> means 'hollow.' For <u>convex</u>, which means 'curved,' I think of the lens of an automobile headlight."

- Max said, "For <u>radius</u>, I think of the spoke of a wheel. The <u>radius</u> is a line from the center of a circle to the outside of it."

- "I know <u>ratio</u>," interrupted Lucy. "The <u>ratio</u>, or proportion, of girls to boys in our class is 3 to 2. There are 3 girls for every 2 boys."

. . . .

In Your Notebook Write each list word and its meaning. Include a small sketch to help you remember each meaning.

Word Roots

Concave and *convex* both have the root *con,* which means "together." *Concave* and *convex* often refer to lenses. As light goes through a lens, it changes directions. A concave lens is thinner in the middle. It causes light rays to spread apart.

con (together) + cavus (hollow) = concave (hollow; curved in)

A convex lens is thicker in the middle. It causes light rays to come together.

con (together) + vehere (to bring) = convex (curved out)

A magnifying glass is a convex lens that makes things look bigger.

Apply and Extend

■ *Compass* sometimes means "limits" or "boundaries," as in, *The prisoner lives within the <u>compass</u> of the walls of his cell.* Write a sentence using one of these meanings.

■ Party hats often are shaped like a *cone* with an elastic strap to hold them on the head. How many other things can you name that have the shape of a cone? You should be able to name at least three.

Rap It Up Working with a classmate, choose a word from the week's lesson. Use the word and its definition to create a short poem or rap, such as the one below. Compile your rap with other classmates' raps into a Rap It Up notebook.

> ### Lenses
> Concave—curved in like a cave.
> Convex—curved out like a bow.
> As I think about a lens,
> This tells me how to go.

doc

Doc is a Latin root that means "teach."

- Words containing *doc* usually have something to do with teaching.

When you see *doc,* think of **doc**umentary (film or television program that "teaches" the facts of an actual event).

LIST 1

docent
docile
doctrine
indoctrinate

Clues to Meaning Use *doc* as a clue to the meanings of the underlined words.

- The museum docent was a volunteer who enjoyed teaching others what she knew about seventeenth century paintings.

- I would prefer to own a docile dog than one that is not obedient.

- Alyssa's parents follow a political doctrine, but Alyssa does not share the same set of beliefs.

- It takes weeks to indoctrinate a new staff writer at the newspaper, training the person in all that needs to be known.

· ·

log

LIST 2

epilogue
illogical
logistically
prologue

Log is a Greek root that means "word."

- Words containing *log* usually have something to do with words, speech, or reasoning.
- The word *dialogue* has a Greek prefix and root.

dia (between) + logue (speech) = dialogue

When you see *log,* think of *dialogue* ("words" between two or more people).

Clues to Meaning Use *log* as a clue to the meanings of the underlined words.

- The book was so good that I read it straight through, from the prologue, the note at the beginning, to the epilogue at the end.

- Because she loves that performer, it's illogical to think that Janice won't want to go to the concert.

- Logistically, this moving plan is a nightmare! It's just not organized!

· ·

LIST 3 anti

antidote
antigen
antipathy
antiphonal

Anti is a Greek prefix that means "against."
- Words beginning with *anti* usually relate to being against or opposing something.

ANCHOR WORD
antibacterial

When you see *anti,* think of **anti**bacterial (something that is "against" bacteria and counteracts or destroys them).

Clues to Meaning Use *anti* as a clue to the meanings of the underlined words.

- <u>Antigens</u>, such as pollens, invade your body and can make you sick. Your immune system produces antibodies, which are the best <u>antidote</u> for fighting off illness.

- The feuding between the Hatfields and the McCoys, caused by the <u>antipathy</u>, the strong feelings, that each family felt against the other, finally came to an end in 1891 when the families agreed to a truce.

- <u>Antiphonal</u> chanting, in which one person or group prays or sings and another person or group answers, is usually associated with church music.

• •

In Your Notebook Write each list word and its meaning. Write a context clue next to each that will help you remember the words' meanings. If you need to check a meaning, use a dictionary.

Word Roots

The family of words based on the root *log* is large. One form, *ology,* means "the study of" or "the science of." You probably are familiar with many of the words formed with this root. *Psychology,* the study of the mind, was new in the seventeenth century, when the science was just beginning. *Geology,* the study of the Earth, developed about 100 years later, and *ecology,* the study of the environment, entered the language in 1873. Think about what the following branches of science might study: *urbanology, astrobiology, primatology, garbology.* Use a dictionary or online resource to find out when these words were first used. What does this tell you about these sciences?

■ List 1

Write a sentence or two using all four list words. Be creative!

■ List 2

How are *epilogue* and *prologue* related in meaning? Write a sentence with each word, using context that shows you understand their meanings.

■ List 3

Write a question about one of the words that contains *anti,* showing that you understand the meaning of the word. An example question for the word *antipathy* is: *Which word describes a person's strong negative feelings for another?*

Clue Review Play a word game with one of your classmates. Choose one of the list words. Give your partner a clue about the word. Did your partner guess the word correctly? If not, provide another clue until your partner correctly identifies the word. Then switch roles.

Did you know?

You can hear *antiphonal,* or call-and-response, singing in blues, gospel, and rock-and-roll music.

LIST WORDS

complacent
despondent
ecstatic
exuberance
exultantly
forlorn
jubilation
melancholy

Use Context as Clues to Meaning

The English language is rich with words that writers use to express joy and sorrow and every shade of emotion in between. When writing about a character's emotions, a writer might use dialogue or give a detailed description of the character's feelings.

Compare these paragraphs.

> After her dog ran away, LaTonya was very **sad**. Her mood changed, though, when Greg texted her, "I found your dog!" LaTonya was **happy**.

> After her dog ran away, LaTonya was very **despondent**. Her mood changed, though, when Greg texted her, "I found your dog!" LaTonya was **ecstatic**.

Which paragraph conveys LaTonya's emotions more precisely? The word *despondent,* which means "to lose heart, courage, or hope," expresses much more emotion than the word *sad*. And the word *ecstatic,* which means "in high spirits; joyful or proud," expresses much more emotion than the word *happy*.

Read the passage about Mimi's mood. How does the context help you understand the meanings of the underlined words?

Mimi could hear the crowd cheering <u>exultantly</u> and joyfully as she approached the parade. This was supposed to be a wonderful day, but she couldn't shake the gloomy, <u>melancholy</u> mood that had settled over her ever since her best friend, Sammi, had moved away. She remembered how <u>forlorn</u> she felt when Sammi left; she was so alone! In the days after Sammi's departure, Mimi missed their talks and was <u>despondent</u>, in low spirits, and hoped that she would somehow get through the weeks before school without seeing her friend. In a few moments she would have to deal with everyone's <u>exuberance</u> and <u>jubilation</u> at the parade, and she just wasn't sure she could face such happiness in others. The only thing that would make her <u>ecstatic</u> right now—and give her great joy—would be to see Sammi. But she lived 2,000 miles away now, so that was probably not going to happen anytime soon. Even feeling <u>complacent</u> would be a relief—she couldn't even remember what it felt like to be content, or satisfied with something. Anything would be better than this awful loneliness.

In Your Notebook Write the list words. Then, next to each one, write about something that might make you feel that way.

Connotation and Denotation

The literal dictionary meaning of a word is its *denotation*, but many words have the power to suggest or imply a range of meanings, depending on the context and the author's purpose. A word's suggested meaning is its *connotation*—and a connotation can be either positive or negative. For example, one person might interpret someone's jubilation as rejoicing, while another person might interpret that person's jubilation as gloating.

Apply and Extend

□ The list words convey a range of joyful and sad emotions. Which word do you think expresses the most joy? the most sadness? Write a sentence for each of these two words, describing an emotion you have felt.

□ An old German saying reminds us that "Joy and sorrow are next-door neighbors." Write two or three sentences, using list words, to explain what you think this old saying means.

Word History Choose a list word related to joy and one related to sorrow. What can you find out about the history and origins of your two words? Answer the following questions:

- From which language did your words derive?

- What are the first recorded instances of their use in the English language?

- What is one interesting fact you learned about each word?

- List related words that you find.

Did you know?
Forlorn and *lovelorn* ("pining for love") include the same Old English base word, *loren,* which means "to lose."

LIST 1

path

apathy
empathize
pathetic
pathogen
pathologist
pathos

Path is a Greek root that means "feeling," "emotion," "suffer," or "disease."

- Words containing *path* usually have something to do with feelings, suffering, disease, or treatment of disease.
- Use *path* as a clue to meaning when you come across words that contain this root.

When you see *path,* think of *empathy* (to experience another's "feelings" as if they were your own).

Clues to Meaning Use *path* as a clue to the meanings of the underlined words.

Most of George's so-called friends showed nothing but <u>apathy</u> when he fell ill. They didn't seem to have any feelings about it at all. But Alicia could <u>empathize</u>. She had experienced a long illness herself and understood just what George was going through. When George fainted during a 5K race, Henry thought George showed a <u>pathetic</u> need for attention; he thought it was false and pitiable. Alicia, though, saw the <u>pathos</u> in the situation. Her heart went out to George in real pity because he was trying so hard.

Finally, the <u>pathologist</u> who had been looking for the cause of George's illness learned that George's blood contained a high level of a toxin caused by a virus. The doctor began to treat George to remove the <u>pathogen</u> from his body. George made a full recovery.

symbol
symmetric
symptom
synchronize
syntax
synthetic

Sym is a Greek prefix that means "together" or "with." Another way to spell this root is *syn*.

- To figure out words with the prefix *sym* or *syn,* identify the root first and then add the meaning "together" or "with."

- The word *sympathy* has two Greek roots.
  sym (with) + pathos (feeling) = sympathy

When you see *sym* or *syn,* think of **sym**pathy (sharing "with" a person's feeling of sorrow or trouble).

Clues to Meaning Use *sym* and *syn* as clues to the meanings of the underlined words.

- The image of two clasping hands is a <u>symbol</u> for friendship.

- The shape of the starfish was perfectly <u>symmetric</u>: each arm had the same width and length and was spaced evenly around the center.

- A fever can be a <u>symptom</u> of the flu, a sign that comes along with the disease.

- People working together sometimes <u>synchronize</u> their watches before a project so they can start and finish at the same time.

- The sentence had strange <u>syntax</u>: the words were arranged in such a way that it was difficult to understand the writer's meaning.

- <u>Synthetic</u> silk is made artificially rather than from silkworm cocoons.

• •

In Your Notebook Write each list word and its meaning. What context clues helped you figure out word meaning? To check a meaning, use a dictionary.

LESSON 13

Analogy Study

Forming an analogy is one way of comparing or contrasting words or ideas. An analogy is a sentence that has two word pairs, with the same relationship between the items in each pair. You have to think about the relationship between the first pair of words in order to see a relationship between the second pair. Those relationships might be as synonyms, antonyms, parts of a whole, descriptions, and others. For example:

"Real is to artificial as excitement is to _____."

Real and *artificial* are antonyms. Therefore, you need to think about the opposite of *excitement*. *Apathy* is an appropriate word for the blank.

Sometimes an analogy is written with colons, such as this:

real : artificial :: excited : apathy

Did you know?

The words *feeling, suffer,* and *disease* are related. Disease can cause suffering, and *suffering* describes feeling bad. Another person can see the suffering, know deeply what it feels like, and feel pity or tenderness.

Apply and Extend

■ List 1

Write a question about one of the words that contains the root *path,* showing that you understand the meaning of the word. An example question for the word *apathy* is: *Which word describes a lack of feeling?*

■ List 2

Choose two words from the list and write a sentence using both. Provide context that shows you understand the meanings of both words.

■ List 2

Write an analogy using one of the list words and three other words of your choice. The analogy may show antonyms, synonyms, or another relationship. If you need to, use a dictionary or go online to look for words.

Rap It Up Working with a classmate, choose a word from the week's lesson. Use the word and its definition to create a short poem or rap. Compile your rap with other classmates' raps into a Rap It Up notebook.

40

abbreviation
acronym
adage
bibliography
footnote
idiom
oxymoron
palindrome

Use Context as Clues to Meaning

Remember that *syntax* is a word that describes the order of words in a sentence. In fact, language arts uses many other words that simply describe words. For example, the word *acronym* has the Greek roots *acros* ("tip") and *onyma* ("name"). An acronym is a name made from the first letters, or "tips," of other words.

At the right are more words about words. You may come across these words in your language arts class.

How do the following sentences help you understand the meanings of the underlined words?

- The abbreviation for *Doctor* is *Dr.* It is a shortened way of spelling the word.

- An acronym is a word that can be pronounced formed from the "tips"—the first letter or syllable—of other words. *Radar* is an acronym for radio detecting and ranging.

- My grandpa always uses the adage "a penny saved is a penny earned." He quotes this well-known saying to teach me about managing my money.

- The essay included a bibliography, which listed the sources the writer had used.

- Whenever the author quoted a source, she included a footnote, a note at the bottom of the page, to show the page in the source from which the quotation came.

- "To catch a cold" is an idiom that means to become ill with a cold. An idiom is an expression that does not mean exactly what it says; you just have to know what it means.

- *Bittersweet* is an oxymoron because the word suggests two opposite meanings. How can something be both bitter *and* sweet?

- A palindrome, such as "Madam, I'm Adam," reads the same forward and backward. Other short examples are "dad," "peep," and "stats."

In Your Notebook Write each list word and its meaning in your notebook.

Word Story

An oxymoron is a figure of speech in which words are used together even though they have opposite meanings and therefore are contradictory (for example, "jumbo shrimp"). The word *oxymoron* has the Greek roots *oxys* ("sharp") and *moros* ("foolish"). For example, the expression "deafening silence" does not make sense literally but does communicate what it feels like to hear only silence in response to a speech or performance. Some other examples of oxymorons are sad optimist, organized mess, and fiery ice. Can you explain why these expressions are oxymorons?

Did you know?

The word *palindrome* has the Greek roots *palin* ("back") and *dromos* ("a running" or "racecourse"). You can "run back" through a palindrome from the end, and it will read the same way.

Apply and Extend

■ The word *acronym* shares a suffix (Greek *onyma*, "name") with the words *synonym, antonym, homonym,* and *pseudonym.* What do these words mean? How are they related to their suffix? Use a dictionary to answer these questions if you need to.

■ Choose four of the list words and tell when and why you would use what that word refers to or means. For example, when and why would you use a footnote?

Skit Work with several classmates to perform a skit based on the list words in this lesson. Have each person choose a language-arts–related word to act out. For example, several people holding alphabet cards showing a palindrome could then reverse their order to illustrate the meaning of *palindrome.*

hydr	**LIST 1**

hydrate
hydraulic
hydroelectric
hydroplane

Hydr is a Greek root that means "water."

- Words containing *hydr* usually have something to do with water or fluid.
- When you see *hydr,* think of a **hydrant** (a fireplug that firefighters connect "water" hoses to).

Clues to Meaning Use *hydr* as a clue to the meanings of the underlined words.

Teacher Who can tell me what a <u>hydrate</u> is?

Aaron It's a chemical compound formed when water is added to certain chemical substances.

Teacher Can someone tell me how a <u>hydraulic</u> system works?

Maria Pressure on a liquid, either water or oil, in one part of the system causes motion or force in another part of the system.

Teacher Excellent. Now who can tell me what kind of power is generated by the movement of water?

Lee That's <u>hydroelectric</u> power.

Teacher Very good. Who can tell me what a <u>hydroplane</u> is?

Jenna It's a very fast boat that skims across the surface of the water.

Teacher Great job! I think you're all ready for the science quiz!

• •

aqu	**LIST 2**

aquanaut
aquatic
aqueduct
aquifer

Aqu is a Latin root that means "water."

- The word *aquanaut* has two Greek roots
  aqua (water) + naut (sailor) = aquanaut
- When you see *aqu,* think of **aquarium** (a tank with "water" in it).

43

Clues to Meaning Use *aqu* as a clue to the meanings of the underlined words.

- In ancient Rome, a system of aqueducts that looked like channels built on stone and brick stilts carried water throughout the land.

- The well in my yard is a narrow pipe that goes down to the aquifer, a pocket of water that flows between the rocks more than 100 feet below the ground.

- After I went on my first snorkeling trip, I realized that I want to be an aquanaut exploring underwater. Whenever I can, I read about aquatic plants and animals so I can learn about the fascinating life forms that live in the water.

LIST 3

circumnavigation
naval
navigable
navigator

nav

ANCHOR WORD
navy

Nav is a Latin root that means "ship."

- Words containing *nav* usually have something to do with ships.

When you see *nav,* think of **nav**y (the branch of the armed forces involving "ships" and sailors).

Clues to Meaning Use *nav* as a clue to the meanings of the underlined words.

In the 1500s, Ferdinand Magellan's ship, the *Nao Victoria,* became the first vessel to complete a circumnavigation of the Earth. Magellan, a skilled navigator, spent more than three years guiding his ships on their journey around the globe, but he didn't live to see his journey completed. Juan Sebastián Elcano took over after Magellan's death and completed the historic voyage. For any long-distance sea voyage, a captain must carefully plan the route he will follow, and he must make certain that he guides his ships through navigable waters. If he were to mistakenly select dangerous seas or channels that were too shallow, he would risk losing not only his naval fleet but also the lives of the men aboard the ships.

In Your Notebook Write each list word and its meaning.

Synonym Study

Aquatic has the Latin root *aqu,* which means "water." Something that is aquatic occurs or exists in or on water. Some synonyms for *aquatic* are *marine, watery, oceanic, naval, seafaring, submerged, underwater,* and *floating.*

How do you know which synonyms to use in your writing? Use the word that most precisely expresses what you want to say.

Did you know?
The word *hydroplane* used to refer to airplanes that took off and landed from water. *Hydroplane* is also the name of a figure-skating move.

Apply and Extend

■ List 1

Write one sentence for each word in List 1. Make sure that your sentences show that you understand the meanings of the words.

■ List 2

Which of these words do you like the best? Why? Which do you find the least interesting? Why?

■ List 3

Try to use as many of the List 3 words as you can in one sentence. For example: *The <u>navigator</u> will guide the <u>naval</u> fleet through <u>navigable</u> waters on the ships' <u>circumnavigation</u> of the Earth.*

Word History Choose an interesting word from this week's lesson. What can you find out about the history and origins of your word? Answer the following questions:

- From which language did your word derive?
- What is the first recorded instance of its use in the English language?
- What is one interesting fact you learned about the word?
- List related words that you find.

LIST WORDS

bacteria
condense
freshwater
ground water
hydrology
hydrosphere
precipitates
tributary

Use Context as Clues to Meaning

All life forms need access to clean, drinkable water. Most water on Earth is salt water, but living things that live on land can't drink it. For years scientists have tried to make salt water drinkable for humans and animals.

These scientists are involved in the field of hydrology, or the science of water. The word *hydrology* has two parts.

hydr (water) + ology (science of) = hydrology (science of water)

At the left are more words related to water. You may study these words in your science class.

Read about the study of water. How does the context help you understand the meanings of the underlined words?

The <u>hydrosphere</u> is the total amount of water found on the Earth, including the vapor in the air surrounding Earth. It is the salt water in oceans and the <u>freshwater</u> in lakes and rivers. Unlike salt water, <u>freshwater</u> does not contain salt. <u>Ground water</u> is the water that flows downward and seeps into and soaks the soil. Ice, glaciers, and icebergs are frozen water.

To understand <u>hydrology</u>, or the science of water, you need to understand the water cycle. First, water changes from a liquid to a vapor, or evaporates, from oceans, lakes, and rivers. Then it collects in clouds, where it <u>condenses</u>, or changes back to a liquid. Next it falls to Earth as solid substances called <u>precipitates</u>, such as rain, snow, or sleet. <u>Precipitates</u> collect in rivers, lakes, oceans, and <u>tributaries</u>, or streams that flow into the larger bodies of water. Then they evaporate into the atmosphere to start the cycle again. <u>Bacteria</u> are one-celled microorganisms found in nearly all things. Some cause disease, while others are helpful. The water cycle helps bacteria travel through the <u>hydrosphere</u>.

• •

In Your Notebook Write each list word and its meaning. To check a meaning, use a dictionary.

Word Story

The list word *bacteria* is the plural form of *bacterium*, which comes from a Greek word meaning "little rod." There are three kinds of bacteria: bacillus (rod-shaped), coccus (round-shaped), and spirillum (spiral shaped). When scientists first discovered bacteria, they mostly saw the rod-shaped kind and named them after that shape. The word *bacillus* comes from a Latin word that also means "little rod."

Apply and Extend

- Write sentences to explain how *freshwater, ground water,* and *precipitates* are different. You may want to use a dictionary.

- Explain the water cycle by making a diagram of it. Use as many of the list words as you can in your diagram.

Word History Choose an interesting word from this lesson. What can you find out about the history and origins of your word? Answer these questions:

- From which language did your word derive?
- What is the first recorded instance of its use in the English language?
- What is one interesting fact you learned about the word?
- List any related words that you find.

Did you know?

Precipitates comes from a Latin word that means "thrown headlong." The word describes condensed substances, but *precipitates* is also a verb meaning "hastens the beginning of" or "hurls": *She precipitates herself into conversations.*

LIST 1

grammarian
grammatical
graphite
hologram
micrograph
monogram
monograph
topography

graph, gram

Graph is a Greek root that means "write." Another way to spell this root is *gram*.

- Words containing *graph* or *gram* usually have something to do with writing or drawing.
- When you see *graph* or *gram*, think of *autograph* (a person's "written" signature).

Clues to Meaning Use *graph* and *gram* as clues to the meanings of the underlined words.

- My college professor wrote a scholarly article on using <u>micrographs</u> to aid in teaching science. These photographs of tiny objects as seen through a microscope clearly show features of life forms not visible to the eye. The article is a <u>monograph</u> because it is about one topic.

- My sisters and I share a bathroom, so we have always mixed up our towels. Mom has ordered towels with <u>monograms</u>. Carissa's towel will have a *C*, Belinda's will have a *B*, and mine will have an *E* for Eve.

- The label says the <u>graphite</u> pencils are made from a soft, black form of carbon. I'll use it to draw my map of the <u>topography</u> of this area. I must draw its surface features—the hills, streams, and roads.

- On the cover of the birthday card is a <u>hologram</u>, a picture made with a laser. In the light, the picture looks three-dimensional. The letters in the words "Happy Birthday" almost pop off the page. James makes mistakes when he writes sentences—he is no <u>grammarian</u>. He even made a <u>grammatical</u> mistake in the card. Inside, he wrote, "All of us wishes you a Happy Birthday."

forebode
forego
foresight
forewarn

Fore is an Old English prefix that means "before" or "beforehand."

- To figure out words with the prefix *fore,* identify the base word first and then add the meaning "before" or "beforehand."

ANCHOR WORD
forecast

When you see *fore,* think of **fore**cast (say "beforehand," or predict).

Clues to Meaning Use *fore* as a clue to the meanings of the underlined words.

Pauli told us he had foresight and could tell the future. Early in the school year, he predicted that our class would forego our class trip. First, he forebode that it would rain during our trip. "Be forewarned!" he cautioned. "There will be thunderstorms that day!" After weeks of his annoying warnings, the class agreed to cancel the trip. We gave the money to a local food pantry instead. Pauli happily reminded us that he had forecasted what happened. We told him he made it happen by being such a nuisance!

• •

In Your Notebook Write each list word and its meaning. If you need to check a meaning, use a dictionary.

Using a Thesaurus

A thesaurus can help you better understand a word. Like a dictionary, a thesaurus lists entry words in alphabetical order.

For each entry word, thesauruses list synonyms, or words with similar meanings. For example, synonyms for *forego* include *refrain* and *withhold*. Antonyms, or words with opposite meanings, include *give in* and *submit*.

In your writing, use a thesaurus to find synonyms and antonyms that express the meaning of what you want to say in a precise, exact way.

Apply and Extend

Did you know?

The prefix *fore* has a meaning other than "before." It can also mean "front of" or "at the front," as in the words *forehead, forefront,* and *foreground.*

■ List 1

Think about how *grammatical, topography, micrograph,* and *monograph* are related in meaning. Should a monograph be grammatical? Can it be about micrographs or topography? Write a sentence or two using these words.

■ List 1

Write a question about one of the list words. Show that you understand the meaning of the word. An example question for the word *grammarian* is: *Which word describes a person who is an expert in using a language correctly?*

■ List 2

The words *forebode, forego,* and *forewarn* are related in meaning but have key differences. Write a few sentences explaining the differences in the meanings of these words.

Rap It Up Working with a classmate, choose a word from the week's lesson. Use the word and its definition to create a short poem or rap. Compile your rap with other classmates' raps into a Rap It Up notebook.

> **Foresight**
> My foresight has never mislead me, nope.
> I'll spot clues that help me figure out the likely scenario.
> Is that a big patch of gray I see in the sky?
> Forego that picnic! Don't go. Don't even try.
> Did our favorite team win the last two games?
> I'm sure they'll win the next one if they keep the same players in play.
> Don't expect me to waste my money on silly things!
> I have enough foresight to use my money wisely!

endorse
filibuster
government
legislator
political party
reconcile
representative
subsidize

Use Context as Clues to Meaning

Does anyone in your family benefit from a government program? Probably. Government programs are plans written by legislators that help citizens in many ways, such as providing funds for school lunches.

The word *program* has the Greek root *gram,* which means "write," and the prefix *pro,* which means "forth." The word *legislator* comes from a Latin word that means "proposer of a law."

pro (forth) + gram (write) = program (write forth a plan)

legis (law) + lator (proposer) = legislator (proposer of a law)

At the right are more words related to government, the form of rule a country has. You may study these words in your social studies class.

Read these paragraphs about the U.S. government. How does the context help you understand the meanings of the underlined words?

Every four years, U.S. citizens vote for a President. Most people who run for President belong to a <u>political party</u>, a group of people with common beliefs about issues facing the country. Often, those in a <u>political party</u> <u>endorse</u>, or support, the person from their party who is running for office.

Citizens also vote for <u>legislators</u>, such as senators and <u>representatives</u>, who come from their states and are responsible for making laws. After the President and <u>legislators</u> are elected, they talk about possible laws. For example, they might write a law allowing the <u>government</u> to <u>subsidize</u>, or give money to, a new school program. When writing a law, everyone can voice an opinion about how the law will be worded. Then all of the opinions are brought together, or <u>reconciled</u>, into one document. Sometimes a <u>legislator</u> feels so strongly that a law is not yet worded right that he or she will <u>filibuster</u>, deliberately making a long speech or doing something else in order to delay the vote.

• •

In Your Notebook Write the list words. Then choose two words and make a 4-square concept map for each word. Include context that shows you understand the word's meaning.

Synonym Study

Endorse comes from Latin and means "to approve."

en (on) + dors (back) = endorse

If you endorse a person, you "back" him or her. To endorse a check, you write your name on the back of it to assure its payment. You are standing in "back" of it, or "approving" its transfer to you. Some synonyms for *endorse* are *approve, support, back, favor, recommend, uphold, authorize,* and *confirm.* You can use a thesaurus to find synonyms. When you are writing, a thesaurus is a useful reference for finding a word with the exact meaning you want to communicate.

Did you know?

The word *filibuster* has its roots in a Spanish word for "pirate" and the Dutch words for "stolen valuables." A legislator in a filibuster "seizes" possession of a legislature's processes.

Apply and Extend

- Which list word or words have been in the news recently? Write what you are hearing about them.

- *Representatives,* those who represent the people, usually come from *political parties.* A *political party* is a group of people who share the same views about the way power should be used. Name two other issues on which representatives from the same party would likely agree.

Clue Review Play a word game with one of your classmates. Choose one of the list words. Give your partner a clue about the word. Did your partner guess the word correctly? If not, provide another clue until your partner correctly identifies the word. Then switch roles.

vac	**LIST 1**

List 1

evacuate
vacancy
vacate
vacation
vacuity
vacuous
vacuum

Vac is a Latin root that means "empty."

- Words containing *vac* usually have something to do with being empty or not filled.
- When you see *vac,* think of **vac**ant ("empty" or unoccupied).

Clues to Meaning Use *vac* as a clue to the meanings of the underlined words.

Violet Hey, Venus, are you back from <u>vacation</u> already? How was your trip?

Venus Interesting, to say the least! We were away from home on a visit to a very pretty island. But we had to <u>evacuate</u> the island because of a big storm. We left it by boat and headed to the nearest mainland.

Violet Wow! Was it scary?

Venus Yes! We were among the last to <u>vacate</u>. Almost everyone had already left. The place we were taken to was jammed with people—there wasn't a hotel <u>vacancy</u> anywhere—and then suddenly everyone was gone. The resort was so empty, it was like a <u>vacuum</u>.

Violet And you thought you were going to have a <u>vacuous</u> time just hanging out on the beach doing nothing.

Venus No kidding. Instead of a little time off and mental <u>vacuity</u>—and I was really looking forward to having nothing to think about—we had way too much excitement. I need a <u>vacation</u> from my <u>vacation</u>!

• •

cipher	**LIST 2**

List 2

cipher
ciphered
decipherment
encipher
indecipherable

Cipher is a Latin root that means "code."

- Words containing *cipher* usually have something to do with a code.
- *Cipher* is a root; *cipher* is also a word with a similar meaning to the root.
- When you see *cipher,* think of *de**cipher*** (to figure out a "code").

Clues to Meaning Use *cipher* as a clue to the meanings of the underlined words.

For forty years, numbers stations—shortwave radio stations—have continuously broadcast lists of numbers and words, and even some music. Radio buffs and secret code enthusiasts around the world can't crack these <u>ciphers</u>; the codes have been <u>indecipherable</u>. Without the <u>decipherment</u> of any messages, experts don't know what the messages say. However, they believe that each country's broadcasts contain instructions to spies. To <u>encipher</u> messages takes a "one-day pad," which contains a code good for one day. Once encoded, the messages are broadcast to spies in the field who are awaiting assignments. You can learn more about these mysterious <u>ciphered</u> messages on the Internet.

• •

In Your Notebook Write each list word and its meaning. What context clues helped you figure out the word's meaning?

Context Clues

Remember that you can determine a word's meaning by checking its context. Does the text around the word provide any clues? For example, take the sentence, "To <u>encipher</u> messages takes a 'one-day pad,' which contains a code good for one day." If you are uncertain of the word *encipher*, continue reading: "Once encoded, the messages are broadcast. . . ." Both *encipher* and *encoded* refer to what must happen to the messages before they are sent. You can figure out from this that *encode* must be a synonym for *encipher*. The context clue has helped you solve the mystery. You can use a dictionary to confirm that you have deciphered the word correctly.

Apply and Extend

■ List 1

Both *vacuum* and *vacation* can be used as either nouns or verbs. Write sentences using each as both parts of speech.

■ List 2

The word *cipher* has several meanings. Look up the meanings of *cipher* and write two sentences using *cipher*, each showing a different meaning.

■ List 2

Several words in this list include prefixes that change the meaning of *cipher*. Identify each, write the words, and write what they mean.

Act It Out Put your acting talent to work! Work with classmates to write and perform a skit based on the List 1 passage. Add more characters to the skit who talk about their vacations.

Did you know?
Before the Latin word was used, *cipher* came from the Arabic word *sifr,* meaning "zero." Later, *cipher* came to mean any number. Because many codes substitute numbers for letters, it soon meant "code."

LIST WORDS

acute
angle
apex
arc
circular
coordinate
intersect
obtuse

Use Context as Clues to Meaning

Geometry, one branch of mathematics, started out in the ancient world as the science of measuring land. The word *geometry* has two Greek roots. *Geo* means "Earth." *Metry* comes from *metron,* meaning "measure." At the left are more words related to geometry. You may come across these words in your math class.

The word *intersect* has the Latin prefix *inter* and the root *sect,* from the Latin root *secare.*

inter (between) + sect (cut) = intersect

Read about geometry. How do the context and illustrations help you understand the meanings of the underlined words?

Geometry is the mathematical study of shapes, points, lines, surfaces, and <u>angles</u>, or figures formed when two lines meet. Lines can <u>intersect</u> (cut or cross) one another or be parallel. When lines meet, they can form wide, <u>obtuse</u> angles or narrow, <u>acute</u> ones. <u>Coordinates</u> on a grid are a pair of numbers that show the point where two lines meet.

The circumference of a <u>circular</u>, or round, shape is the distance around it. An <u>arc</u> is a part of that circumference.

The <u>apex</u> of a triangle or a pyramid is the highest point, opposite the base.

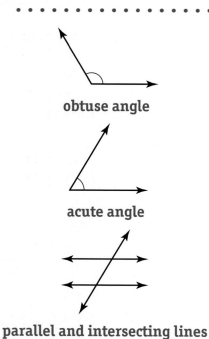

obtuse angle

acute angle

parallel and intersecting lines

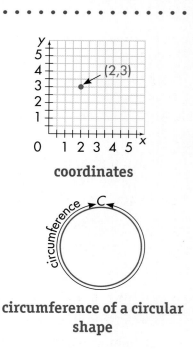

coordinates

circumference of a circular shape

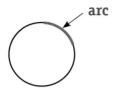 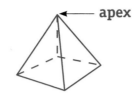

arc   apex

. . . .

In Your Notebook Write each list word and its meaning. You may want to use a sketch to illustrate a word's meaning.

Multiple Meanings

The words in this lesson have meanings that are related to geometry. However, they also have more general meanings. In many cases, the mathematical meaning and the general meaning of a word are related and likely come from the same root. For instance, *acute* can mean sharp, as in a sharp pain. Think about an acute angle: it is sharp. *Obtuse*, on the other hand, can mean blunt, or not sharp. How is this sense reflected in an *obtuse* angle? A dictionary will list the multiple meanings of words.

> **Have you heard these expressions?**
> - looking at something from a different angle
> - circular reasoning
> - streets that intersect

Apply and Extend

■ The word *coordinate* has several meanings and can function as different parts of speech. *Coordinate* also has two different pronunciations, depending on its part of speech. Write three sentences: one using *coordinate* as related to math, one using it as a verb, and one using it as a noun. You may want to consult a dictionary.

■ Choose a shape. Use as many of the list words as you can to describe it. For example, describe its shape, measurements, angles, lines, and/or points.

Word History Choose an interesting word from this lesson. What can you find out about the history and origins of your word?

- From what language did your word derive?
- What is the first recorded instance of its use in English?
- What is one interesting fact you learned about the word?
- List related words that you find.

LIST 1

dem

demagogue
demographics
endemic
epidemic
epidemiology

ANCHOR WORD
democracy

Dem is a Greek root that means "people."

- Words containing *dem* usually have something to do with people.
- When you see *dem,* think of **dem**ocracy (rule by the "people").

Clues to Meaning Use *dem* as a clue to the meanings of the underlined words.

- An <u>epidemic</u> is an illness that spreads very quickly.

- Avian flu is <u>endemic</u> to the poultry in six countries, where the disease is regularly found. It has not yet spread around the world.

- A country's <u>demographics</u> are the facts about its people, such as the population, where they live, and the number of births and deaths.

- <u>Epidemiology</u> is the study of diseases and how they spread within a community.

- A <u>demagogue</u> is a leader who makes speeches to stir up the country's people, getting them to do what he or she wants.

LIST 2

bio

biochemistry
biodegradable
biome
biosphere

ANCHOR WORD
biology

Bio is a Greek root that means "life."

- Words containing *bio* usually have something to do with life.
- When you see *bio,* think of **bio**logy (the study of "living" things).

Clues to Meaning Use *bio* as a clue to the meanings of the underlined words.

I want to study <u>biochemistry</u> to learn about what living things are made of. Studying Earth's <u>biomes</u> will help me understand its major systems such as rain forests. I hope to develop <u>biodegradable</u> materials for packaging, such as snack wrappers, that will break down into substances that support life. If I create these materials in every <u>biome</u> type in Earth's <u>biosphere</u>, living things will have a clean, healthy environment instead of a polluted one.

zo

protozoan
zodiac
zoology

Zo is a Greek prefix that means "animal."

- Words containing *zo* usually have something to do with animals.

When you see *zo,* think of **zoo** (a place where "animals" are kept and shown).

Clues to Meaning Use *zo* as a clue to the meanings of the underlined words.

- I love learning about animals, so I want to study <u>zoology</u>.

- <u>Protozoans</u> are tiny forms of life, such as amoebas, that you can see only with a microscope.

- The <u>zodiac</u> is an imaginary belt of stars in the heavens around Earth. Ancient Greeks thought of these stars as being in twelve groups, or constellations.

In Your Notebook Write each list word and a clue to help you remember it.

Using a Dictionary

A dictionary provides different information about a word, such as multiple meanings, which appear in a numbered list; prefixes and suffixes and their meanings; and its etymology, or word history. For example, a dictionary lists two definitions for the word *epidemic:* "the rapid spread of a disease" and "the rapid spread of an idea." It can also tell you more about the word's history. The word *epidemic* comes from Greek words that literally mean "among people." An *epidemic* spreads among people, affecting anyone.

Apply and Extend

Did you know?

The word *zoo* is short for "zoological garden." The name comes from the Zoological Gardens of the London Zoological Society, established in 1828 in Regent's Park to house the society's collection of wild animals.

■ List 1

Pretend you are a demagogue. What might you say about demographics? about an epidemic? Write a few sentences intended to stir up people by appealing to their emotions. Use as many list words as you can.

■ List 2

The List 2 words have the Greek root *bio*. What are two more words with this root? If you want, use a dictionary or go online. Write a sentence for each word, using context clues that explain the word's meaning.

■ List 3

Write one sentence using the List 3 words. Challenge yourself. Can you use all three words in one sentence?

Clue Review Play a word game with one of your classmates. Choose one of the list words. Give your partner a clue about the word. Did your partner guess the word correctly? If not, provide another clue until your partner correctly identifies the word. Then switch roles.

LIST WORDS

capricious
conciliatory
contempt
melee
mollify
pacify
recoil
refute

Use Context as Clues to Meaning

Demographics, or data about the general population and particular groups within it, provide important information about many things, one of them being conflict. Imagine two neighborhoods that border each other and have different cultural, political, and economic characteristics. Such differences are real and might lead to conflict of one kind or another.

Conflict and conflict resolution are concepts that are important in any academic, or educational, area that focuses on people.

Read the passage below. How does the context help you understand the meanings of the underlined words?

"Jorge, that's the fourth idea for a group project you've come up with. You're being underline_capricious! Pick a project already!"

Jorge knew Evita was upset with him, so he tried to be conciliatory. "I guess the one thing I'm certain about," he said, "is that I don't know which idea I like best."

Evita did not respond to Jorge's attempt to make peace. Instead, she looked at him with contempt, as if he were something disgusting on the bottom of her shoe!

"Calm down," Jorge said, trying again to mollify her. "I've made up my mind. Feel better?"

Frankie, who had been quiet until now, jumped in to try to pacify Evita. "Chill out," he said. "We're going to pick a topic and do a great project together."

But you could see Evita physically recoil. As she stepped back, she almost bumped her head on the wall behind her.

"You always take his side!" she cried.

Frankie didn't agree and wanted to refute this statement, but he couldn't think of a way to convince Evita that she was wrong. Once she made up her mind to be mad, she could drag everyone into a big melee. Everyone would end up fighting with everybody else, and no one would even remember what started it all.

"I know," said Jorge. "Let's do our project on conflict!"

• •

In Your Notebook Choose four of the list words and write a few sentences for each one describing a specific behavior to which the word could apply—or, perhaps, has applied in your own life.

English Words from Other Languages

Conflict has taken many forms throughout history, and there are many names for it. Some of these terms, which come from foreign languages, are used by English speakers today. One of the best known is *pax romana*, a Latin phrase that means "Roman peace." A *pax romana* is a peace that is imposed by force or that comes about as a result of military conquest. Another term is *coup d'état* (which is French for a "shock" or "blow" to the "state"), or simply *coup. Coup* and *coup d'état* describe the action of a government being overthrown from within.

Apply and Extend

■ The words *conciliatory, mollify,* and *pacify* are similar in their meanings. Write a sentence for each word that demonstrates the meaning of that word.

■ *Melee* is one of many words in English for "fight" or "battle." Write a sentence or two that include *melee* and two other list words. Use context to show that you understand the meanings of the three words.

Word History Choose an interesting word from this week's lesson. What can you find out about the history and origins of your word? Answer the following questions:

• From which language did your word derive?

• What is the first recorded instance of its use in the English language?

• What is one interesting fact you learned about the word?

• List related words that you find.

tele

telecast
telecommute
telegenic
telepathy
telephoto
telescope

Tele is a Greek prefix that means "far" or "distant."
- Words containing *tele* usually have something to do with actions that take place at a distance.
- When you see *tele,* think of **tele**vision (device that lets you see things that take place "far" away).

Clues to Meaning Use *tele* as a clue to the meanings of the underlined words.

- When I use my telescope to look at the moon, the details I can see at a distance are incredible. The spots on the moon look so much bigger. However, TV cameras must have a telephoto lens, because when the cameras zoom in on the moon, it looks big, bright, and beautiful—telegenic—just what TV viewers like to see!

- We watched a telecast, a television show, that showed how people can telecommute instead of going to an office to work. They work in their own homes and get paid. What happens when a boss needs a worker to do something right away? My teacher jokes that maybe the boss uses telepathy so she can just think about what she wants and the worker knows!

sol

parasol
solarium
solstice

Sol is a Latin root that means "sun."
- Use *sol* as a clue to meaning when you come across words that contain this root.
- When you see *sol,* think of **sol**ar (having to do with the "sun").

Clues to Meaning Use *sol* as a clue to the meanings of the underlined words.

- Lucy carried a parasol, or light umbrella, for shade.
- The solarium at the back of the house had glass walls on three sides and a glass roof, so you could sit inside and enjoy sunshine.
- The solstice is one of two times of the year when the sun is farthest from the Earth's equator.

LIST 3

umbr

adumbrate
penumbra
umbrage

Umbr is a Latin root that means "shadow" or "shade."

- Words containing *umbr* usually have something to do with a shadow or shade.
- When you see *umbr,* think of **umbrella** (a device that "shades" the user from the sun or rain).

Clues to Meaning Use *umbr* as a clue to the meanings of the underlined words.

You can't see a person's face when the sun is right behind the person. The sun <u>adumbrates</u> the person's face—it only outlines it, producing a faint image—because the front of the person is in a shadow.

It's harder to see people standing under a big, leafy tree because they are standing in the shade cast by the <u>umbrage</u>—the leaves of the tree.

In a solar eclipse, the umbra is the darkest part of the shadow that appears when the Earth blocks the sun's light to the moon. The <u>penumbra</u> is the lighter part of the shadow, outside of the umbra.

• •

In Your Notebook Write each list word and its meaning.

Word Story

The word *solstice* comes from the Latin root *sol* meaning "sun" and the Latin word *sistere* meaning "to stand still." The solstice is one of two times of the year when the sun appears to be the farthest north or south in the sky. For several days around the solstice, the sun appears to stay in a fixed position, or "stand still."

The solstice is caused by the Earth's rotation on its axis, or the imaginary line that runs through the North Pole and South Pole, and the Earth's revolution, or circling, around the sun. As the Earth circles the sun, different parts of the Earth tilt toward or away from the sun.

The summer solstice is when the Northern Hemisphere is tilted most toward the sun. This occurs around June 21, the longest day of the year. The opposite happens around December 21, the winter solstice, which is the shortest day of the year.

Apply and Extend

■ List 1

Imagine you are on the moon preparing to broadcast a television show to Earth. Write about this situation using as many of the list words as you can.

■ List 2

Write a question about one of the words that contains *sol*, showing that you understand the meaning of the word part. An example question for the word *solstice* is: *Which word describes the position of the sun when it reaches its highest and lowest point above the horizon during the year?*

■ List 3

The word *umbrage* has multiple meanings. In this lesson, you learned that you can stand under umbrage, but what does it mean to take umbrage? Check the meanings of *umbrage* in a dictionary. Write two or three sentences that demonstrate different meanings of this word.

Riddle Time Work with a classmate. Use several list words and their meanings to create clever riddles. Challenge other classmates to answer your riddles.

Did you know?

Umbrella, which has the root *umbr* (meaning "shadow" or "shade"), comes from a Latin word that means "sunshade." Umbrellas were invented to protect people from the sun, not the rain.

LIST WORDS

bandwagon
contradiction
endorsement
explicit
fallacy
implicit
non sequitur
post hoc

Use Context as Clues to Meaning

We need information in our daily lives, and communication—through the Internet, television, telephone, or the printed word—is an important way to get that information. Sometimes people communicate with us to influence how we think or to get us to agree with them. At the left are words about communication, which you may come across in your language arts classes.

Read this information about ways to influence people. How does the context help you understand the meanings of the underlined words?

Gina and Tony both want your endorsement—your approval or support—as they run for student council president. Gina says, "Vote for me because I'm the best!" Gina's statement is explicit, or clear. Tony says, "Everyone is voting for me. Don't be left behind!" Tony's message is implicit, or indirect. He wants you to "jump on the bandwagon"—do something because other people are doing it.

Is it a fallacy—a mistake in reasoning—to say that most people do something because their friends are doing it? In fact, it's easy to offer a contradiction, or disagreement: Most people think for themselves and do what is right for them.

Other fallacies have Latin names. *Post hoc* means "after this." In a *post hoc* fallacy, a person believes that when one event happens after another, the first caused the second. For example, if good things happened to Tony whenever he wore red socks, he might wear red socks on election day, thinking the socks would cause him to win. Another fallacy, a *non sequitur*, means "does not follow." An example of a non sequitur is if Gina said, "If you don't vote for me, you don't like cats." The second part of her statement "does not follow" the first.

Good luck, Gina and Tony. May the best candidate win!

• •

In Your Notebook Write the list words. Next to each word, tell about a time in your own life when you encountered this situation.

English Words from Other Languages

Many English words are based on a root or word part from a foreign language. However, some foreign words and phrases have become part of the English language. You have seen how we can use Latin phrases such as *post hoc* and *non sequitur* to describe fallacies. Other foreign words used in everyday English include *fiasco*, an Italian word meaning "total failure," and *prima donna*, an Italian phrase meaning "temperamental entertainer."

Apply and Extend

- Watch for examples of celebrities giving *endorsements* for products. Think about whether the endorsements are *explicit* ("I use this product!") or *implicit* (a picture of the celebrity wearing or using the product without saying anything about it). Write two sentences about what you see or read.

- Fallacies often connect two unrelated ideas. For example, which fallacy is illustrated by a basketball player always bouncing the ball three times before shooting every free throw? Write a sentence or two that illustrate an example of each fallacy.

Skit Work with several classmates to write and perform a skit that contains several fallacies, such as bandwagon, *post hoc,* and *non sequitur.* Use as many words from this lesson as possible in your skit.

Did you know?
Political candidates once paraded through town riding on a wagon carrying a musical band. To show support for the candidate, people in the crowd would "jump on the bandwagon."

LIST 1

appendage
compensate
dependable
expendable
indispensable
pending
pension
suspenseful

pend, pens

Pend is a Latin root that means "hang," "weigh," or "pay." Another way to spell this root is *pens*.

- Words containing *pend* or *pens* usually have something to do with hanging, weighing, or paying. When you see *pend* or *pens,* think of **pend**ulum (a "weight" that "hangs" from a fixed point and swings in an arc).

Clues to Meaning Use *pend* and *pens* as clues to the meanings of the underlined words.

- The sea spider has numerous <u>appendages</u> attached to its body. One of them, a long tube-like structure that it uses to suck in food, is on its head. Males have an absolutely necessary pair of <u>appendages</u>. These <u>appendages</u> are <u>indispensable</u> because they carry the eggs until the eggs hatch.

- The research staff at the lab have a <u>pending</u> matter to talk over with their managers, but it won't be settled for a week. The outcome is uncertain and waiting is becoming <u>suspenseful</u>, because staff workers are anxious to know what they will be paid under the new contract. Managers have called their workers reliable, and the workers want to be <u>compensated</u>, or paid well, for being <u>dependable</u>. Management's decision to do away with the <u>pension</u> plan is a problem. The workers want a fixed sum of money on a regular basis after they retire. Their lawyer suggests negotiating for more pay. She says a pension might be <u>expendable</u>, or worth giving up, if salaries are generous enough to allow workers to save money on their own.

LIST 2

salami
saline
salinity
saltwater

sal

Sal is a Latin root that means "salt."

- Words containing *sal* usually have something to do with being salty.
When you see *sal,* think of **sal**t (a seasoning).

Clues to Meaning Use *sal* as a clue to the meanings of the underlined words.

Maria said, "Let's go snorkeling in the ocean. I'd like to see some saltwater fish and plants."

Walking near the ocean's edge, Jordan tripped and went underwater. She came up coughing and said, "The water tastes salty."

"My dad the chemist would say it has salinity," Nia offered.

After they swam, they sat down for lunch. Maria bit into her sandwich and made a face. "This salami is really salty. I don't like such salty meat."

Just then, sand blew into Nia's eye. "Does anyone have saline solution—the salt and water mix I use to rinse my contact lenses?"

• •

In Your Notebook Write each list word and a clue to help you remember it.

Puns

A pun is a play on words. Sometimes the playfulness is based on different meanings of the same word, and other times it is based on words with slightly different sounds. Some puns are silly, and others are clever. Here is a pun using the list word *salami:* "*Jokes about salami are the wurst.*"

This is a pun based on different words that sound the same *(wurst, worst).* The word *wurst* means "sausage," and salami is a type of sausage.

Apply and Extend

■ List 1

Choose two words. Write an example to show you understand the meaning of each word. For example, for *appendage*, you could write *an elephant's trunk* or *a dog's leg*.

■ List 1

Find two words in the list that are antonyms. Write a sentence for each word, using context that demonstrates you understand the meaning of the word.

■ List 2

What do you think of when you think of *saltwater?* Perhaps you think of colorful fish. Write words or phrases that you associate with the list words, but do not write the list words themselves. Exchange your word associations with a partner, and write the list words that match your partner's word associations.

Rap It Up Choose a word from this week's lesson. Use the word and its definition to create a short poem or rap like the one below. Work with classmates to compile the poems and raps into a Rap It Up notebook.

> **Salami**
> Salami is a fun word;
> It's one I like to eat.
> Just put it on some rye bread–
> What a salty treat.

crater
crescent
eclipse
equinox
lunar
observatory
phase
ray

Use Context as Clues to Meaning

In 1969, millions of Americans watched TV in suspenseful silence as two U.S. astronauts stepped off a small spacecraft, called a lunar module, and onto the surface of the moon. The word *lunar* means "of the moon" and is from the Latin *luna* for "moon." At the right are more words related to astronomy, the study of the sun, moon, planets, and stars. You may study these words in your science class.

Read about the moon. How do the context and the illustrations of how the moon is seen from Earth help you understand the meanings of the underlined words?

The moon orbits, or travels around, Earth about every 28 days. From Earth only one side of the moon is ever visible as it goes through eight <u>phases</u>, or stages, as shown in the illustrations below. (The <u>crescent</u> moon, the curved sliver, is the <u>phase</u> most people think of when they think of the moon.) An <u>eclipse</u> occurs when the view of an astronomical body, such as the moon, is temporarily blocked by another astronomical body. For instance, a <u>lunar eclipse</u> occurs when Earth is between the sun and moon and blocks the sun's <u>rays</u>, or beams of light.

The moon has many <u>craters</u>, bowl-shaped holes that cover its surface. The best way to see them is to visit an <u>observatory</u>, a building equipped with a telescope for viewing planets and stars. An <u>observatory</u> is also a good place to view the moon and stars during an <u>equinox</u>, which happens twice a year when the center of the sun crosses the equator and day and night are almost equal in length. The spring <u>equinox</u> occurs about March 20, and the autumnal <u>equinox</u> happens about September 22.

new moon   new crescent   first quarter   waxing gibbous   full moon   waning gibbous   last quarter   old crescent

In Your Notebook Write each list word and its meaning.

71

Using a Glossary

When you are reading a book about a particular subject, such as astronomy, you may come across technical or difficult words. Often you can look up these words in the book's glossary. It usually is at the end of the book and consists of a list of words related to the subject. For example, you would likely find many of the words in this lesson in the glossary of an astronomy book. You will probably find the words listed in alphabetical order, and they will have explanations or comments. The entry may also list the number of the page on which the term appears in the book.

Did you know?

In Roman mythology, Luna was a goddess worshipped during the new moon and the full moon. Temples were built in Rome to honor her.

Apply and Extend

■ This lesson presents the meanings of *eclipse, phase,* and *ray* as used in science. Do you know other meanings for these words? Write a sentence for each word, using context that clearly demonstrates one of the word's meanings. You may want to consult a dictionary.

■ In a *lunar eclipse,* Earth is between the sun and the moon. What happens during a *solar eclipse?* Write a sentence or two explaining the difference between a lunar eclipse and a solar eclipse. You may need to look up *solar eclipse* in a reference book or on the Internet. Remember to use only reliable websites.

■ Look up the etymology of the word *equinox.* In a sentence or two, explain how the word's history relates to its meaning in astronomy.

Clue Review Play a word game with one of your classmates. Choose one of the list words. Give your partner a clue about the word. Did your partner guess the word correctly? If not, provide another clue until your partner correctly identifies the word. Then switch roles.

chron LIST 1

anachronism
chronic
chronicle
chronological
chronology

Chron is a Greek root that means "time."

- Words containing *chron* usually have something to do with time.
- When you see *chron,* think of *syn**chron**ize* (make things agree in "time").

Clues to Meaning Use *chron* as a clue to the meanings of the underlined words.

"What a movie!" Bettina told Alphonse. "And what characters! I thought Leon was the most interesting. At first I didn't realize that he was a <u>chronic</u> liar, just lying all the time. Also," Bettina continued, "there was a time flaw in the plot. It was an <u>anachronism</u> to show Leon on a cell phone. Cell phones hadn't been invented yet."

"Did you follow the order of events before his escape?" Alphonse asked. Bettina thought she understood the <u>chronology</u> of what happened until the two tried to sequence the events in <u>chronological</u> order.

"Let's reread the movie review," Bettina said. "The movie is based on a true story, and the review gives a clear <u>chronicle</u>, or record, of the events that really happened."

. . . .

therm LIST 2

geothermal
thermal
thermos

Therm is a Greek root that means "heat."

- Words containing *therm* usually have something to do with heat, warmth, or temperature.
- When you see *therm,* think of ***therm**ometer* (an instrument for measuring "heat" and cold).

Clues to Meaning Use *therm* as a clue to the meanings of the underlined words.

- Ling stashed the <u>thermos</u> in her backpack; the container of hot cider would taste good later.
- Shivering on the sailboat's cold, wet deck, Tomas wished his raingear had a <u>thermal</u> lining for greater warmth.
- Kimi's house made electricity from solar energy and drew <u>geothermal</u> heat from within the Earth.

. . . .

LESSON 27

LIST 3

cand

candid
candidate
candor
incandescent

Cand is a Latin root that means "shine."

- Words containing *cand* usually have something to do with shining or light.
- When you see *cand,* think of **cand**le (a stick of wax with a wick that "shines" light when burned).

Clues to Meaning Use *cand* as a clue to the meanings of the underlined words.

- She praised the <u>candidate</u> for his <u>candor</u>, wishing that everyone running for office could be so honest in their opinions.

- Mia looked <u>incandescent</u> in her glowing white gown. Her <u>candid</u> speech reminded everyone of her willingness to say what she means.

• •

In Your Notebook Write each list word and its meaning. Think about the context clues that helped you figure out each meaning.

Synonym Study

Candor and *candid* both have to do with saying what you mean and being honest. Be careful, though, because *candor* is a noun and *candid* is an adjective. *Candor* and *candidness* (the noun form of *candid*) are synonyms—words with the same or similar meanings. But even synonyms can have different nuances, or shades of meaning. For example, other synonyms for *candor* and *candidness—directness, fairness,* and *frankness*—have slightly different meanings. How do you know which synonym to use? Think about the precise meaning you want to convey. Then check the word and its definition in a dictionary.

■ List 1

The word *chronicle* can be used as a noun or a verb. Write a sentence for each use of the word, providing context that shows that you understand the meaning.

■ List 2

Write a sentence or two about being in Alaska in a blizzard. Use as many of the list words as you can.

■ List 3

Do you think candidates should be candid? Write two or three sentences explaining why or why not.

Word Part Invention How much of a wordsmith are you? With a partner, combine word parts from this lesson with other letters or syllables to invent a new word. Then write a definition for the word based on the meanings of the word parts. Share the word and definition with classmates.

Did you know?
Candidate comes from *candidus*, Latin for "white," and has the root *cand* (meaning "shine"). Candidates running for office in ancient Rome were distinguished by the white togas they wore.

LIST WORDS

auxiliary
calligraphy
cuneiform
hieroglyphics
papyrus
parchment
pictograph
utensil

Use Context as Clues to Meaning

Around 430 B.C., the Greek writer Herodotus published his chronicle of the wars that had taken place between Greece and Persia years before. (A chronical is a record of events told in order. It contains the Greek root *chron,* which means "time.") He had no computer or software, or even a pen. Instead, he wrote his chronology, titled *Histories,* on ancient paper called *papyrus.*

Ancient Egyptians, Romans, and Greeks wrote on papyrus, and we still have some bits of it today. The words *papyrus* and *paper* come from the same Greek root, *papyros,* which refers to a family of plants from which paper can be made. Before that, the word can be traced to Egypt, where the plant grows. At the left are more words related to the tools and symbols used in writing, such as *calligraphy.* You may come across these words in your social studies class.

The word *calligraphy* has two Greek roots, *kallos* and *graphein.*

kallos (beauty) + graphein (to write) = calligraphy

Read about the first written records. How does the context help you understand the meanings of the underlined words?

While Stone Age cultures covered walls and rocks with drawings called pictographs, the first writing systems appeared in Mesopotamia about 5,000 years ago. Many cultures there wrote with characters called cuneiform, impressing clay with wedge-shaped utensils, the small hand-tools they used. This was a far cry from the calligraphy, or beautiful handwriting, we know today. At the same time, ancient Egyptians painted tomb walls and monuments with symbols called hieroglyphics. They used an auxiliary, or supporting, script called *hieratic* for keeping chronicles on papyrus, an ancient paper. As the reeds to make papyrus grew scarce, parchment, a different kind of paper made from animal skin, began to take its place. What were the first things people wrote? Poems? Love letters? No, they kept accounts and records.

• •

In Your Notebook   Write each list word and its meaning. You may want to draw a picture or your own hieroglyphic (symbol) to define the word.

Context Clues

Remember, the words and sentences around a word you don't know can help you figure out its meaning. One thing to look for is contrast. Words and phrases such as *however, in contrast to, while, but,* and *on the other hand* let you know that one phrase is going to contrast with the other. In the sentence below, the word *while* signals that the second phrase will provide a contrast or comparison with the first.

> While Stone Age cultures covered walls and rocks with <u>pictographs</u>, the first true writing systems appeared as cities developed in Mesopotamia about 5,000 years ago.

From this sentence, you can figure out that pictographs were not true writing systems and therefore must have been other kinds of images or symbols.

Did you know?

The word *hieroglyphics* comes from the Greek words *hieros* meaning "sacred" and *glyphe* meaning "carving." Hieroglyphics were called "sacred carvings" because Ancient Greeks believed only priests could read the "secret" writing.

Apply and Extend

- Choose a list word and write a sentence for it, but do not write in the word. Be sure to use context as clues to the word's meaning. Switch sentences with a partner and supply each other's words.

- Some list words are what you write; some are tools you use when writing. Sort the words into two categories—the symbols and the tools. Select a word from each category and write a sentence that uses both words.

Graphic Gallery Use your skills as a cartoonist to create a comic strip using words from this lesson. Draw pictures and write dialogue or use an online program to create the graphic text. How many of the words can you use? Compile the class's comic strips into a Graphic Gallery.

LIST 1

leg

illegitimate
legalistic
legalize
legislative
legislature
privilege

Leg is a Latin root that means "law."

- Words containing *leg* usually have something to do with law.
- The word *legal* has a Latin root and a Latin suffix.

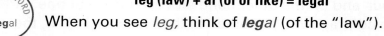

leg (law) + al (of or like) = legal

When you see *leg,* think of *legal* (of the "law").

Clues to Meaning Use *leg* as a clue to the meanings of the underlined words.

Mr. McMurphy's company appeared to be legal. He had all the contracts, licenses, and financial records that were required by law. However, any honest lawyer who looked at McMurphy's records with a <u>legalistic</u> eye, an eye for the law, would find that many of the documents were fake. McMurphy's business was actually <u>illegitimate</u>. Though his company was not legal, it took a <u>legislative</u> action by lawmakers to put McMurphy out of business. The group of lawmakers in the national <u>legislature</u> decided to <u>legalize</u> the use of high-tech snooping devices to use in investigations. As soon as Congress made them lawful, the FBI used their new <u>privilege</u>, this new special right, to get enough proof to end McMurphy's business.

LIST 2

jur, jud, jus

injure
judicial
judicious
jurisdiction
justify
perjury

Jur is another Latin root that means "law." Other spellings for this root are *jud* and *jus*.

- Use *jur, jud,* and *jus* as clues to meaning when you come across words that contain this root.

When you see *jur, jud,* or *jus,* think of *jury* (people who hear evidence and give a decision in a court of "law").

Clues to Meaning Use *jur, jud,* and *jus* as clues to the meanings of the underlined words.

Because he broke federal laws, Mr. McMurphy's case came under the jurisdiction, or the control, of the Ninth Federal Circuit Court, where his trial took place. At the trial, McMurphy swore that he had never injured anyone.

"You have so hurt people! Don't lie in court, Mr. McMurphy, or you'll add perjury to your other crimes," said Judge Fairplay. "You can't justify your actions by explaining them away."

"I tell you, I'm innocent!" shouted McMurphy.

"Nevertheless, after a fair trial, the judicial system has found you guilty," said the judge. "You're a bad man, Mr. McMurphy."

"But I can give you reasons to justify what I did."

"No, Mr. McMurphy," replied Judge Fairplay. "I have made a careful, fair, judicious decision."

• •

In Your Notebook Write the list words. Next to each word, write a simple definition for it based on the story.

Antonym Study

Some list words having to do with the law have antonyms formed by adding or removing the *in/il* prefix, which means "not." For example, an antonym for *legal,* the base word for *legalistic* and *legalize,* is *illegal.* An antonym for *illegitimate* is *legitimate.* An antonym for *judicious* is *injudicious.* Other antonyms for list words or closely related forms are *nonjudicial* and *unjustified.*

Apply and Extend

Have you heard these expressions?

The Latin expression *de jure*, which means "in law," has become part of the English language. It is often used in conjunction with *de facto*, which means "in practice."

■ List 1

In this lesson, the Latin root *leg* means "law." However, there is another Latin root also spelled *leg*, that means "read." This is the root on which the words *legend, legendary,* and *legible* are based. Write two sentences, one using a word with the "law" root and one using a word with the "read" root. Include context that explains the meaning of the word.

■ List 1

The base word of *legalistic* and *legalize* is *legal.* Write a few sentences to explain how the suffixes affect the meaning of *legal* in the words *legalistic* and *legalize.*

■ List 2

Choose two words from the list. Use one word in a question and the other word in an answer to the question. Here is an example: *Q–Why did the judicial system find Mr. McMurphy guilty? A–Because he couldn't justify his actions.*

Act It Out Put your writing and acting talent to work. Work with several classmates to write and perform a skit about Mr. McMurphy and his illegitimate company based on the conversations in this lesson. Include dialogue and action about how he was caught and about the judicial proceedings in his trial. Include additional characters, such as witnesses, to those in this lesson.

approximate
coordinate plane
deviation
dot plot
hyperbola
reciprocal
scatter plot
statistic

Use Context as Clues to Meaning

Do opposites really attract? When two things are the opposite of each other in some way, they are called *reciprocals*. In mathematics, two numbers are *reciprocals* when they equal 1 when multiplied together.

At the right are more words connected with mathematical relationships. You may study these words in your math class.

Read the following math information. How do the context and illustrations help you understand the meanings of the underlined words?

Approximate means "almost or close to." The number 3.9 has the approximate value of 4.0—it is almost 4.0.

A statistic is any fact that can be represented by a number. According to statistics, most people prefer plain cheese pizza to pepperoni.

Graphs can be drawn on a coordinate plane, a flat area formed by the intersection of a horizontal number line and a vertical number line. The graph at the right shows a hyperbola, a pair of curves that are mirror images of each other. The hyperbola includes the number pair 2 and $\frac{1}{2}$, which are reciprocals because the product is equal to 1.

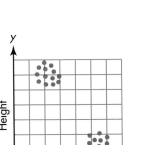

In a deviation graph, each value is shown in relation to a set value, which is zero. It shows how far away a number is from zero.

A dot plot shows a dot on a simple chart to represent information. For example, a dot plot could use dots to represent twelve students' favorite kind of ice cream.

A scatter plot shows a dot on a graph that represents two kinds of information. This scatter plot shows the height and weight of a group of people at a doctor's office. Half were tall and thin, and the other half were shorter and heavier.

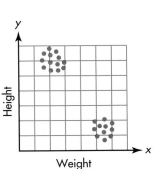

In Your Notebook Write each list word and its meaning. How did the context help you figure out the words' meanings?

Multiple Meanings

In addition to their meanings in mathematics, several list words also have general definitions. For example, the word *deviation* can mean "the act of turning aside from a rule or way," as in this sentence. *Having band practice at 6:00 is a <u>deviation</u> from our usual schedule.*

The word *reciprocal* can mean "in return" or "mutual" as in these sentences.
My sister helped me with my chores, so I gave her <u>reciprocal</u> help. Both employees worked well together because they had <u>reciprocal</u> respect.

When you encounter a multiple-meaning word in a passage, use the context of the sentence to determine which meaning to use. Try each definition in the sentence and choose the meaning that best fits the context.

Apply and Extend

■ Look up the word *approximate*. When it is a verb, is it pronounced the same as or different from the pronunciation when it is an adjective? *Approximate* comes from the Latin word *proximus* meaning "nearest." Write one sentence using *approximate* as a verb and another sentence using it as an adjective.

■ The word *plot* has multiple meanings. Write three sentences using *plot*—one sentence that uses a math meaning and two sentences that use other meanings. Include context that clearly demonstrates the meaning of the word as you intended in each sentence.

The Illustrated Word Sharpen your pencils—it's time to play a picture game. Divide a group into two teams. Write lesson words on cards and place them in a stack upside down. The first person on Team 1 takes a card, draws a picture that represents the word on the card, and shows the picture to his or her team. If team members guess the word in 30 seconds, the team gets a point. Now it's Team 2's turn.

clud, clus | LIST 1

conclude
exclusive
inclusion
inconclusive
occlude
preclude
recluse
seclusion

Clud is a Latin root that means "close" or "shut." Another way to spell this root is *clus*.

- Words containing *clud* or *clus* usually have something to do with shutting or closing.
- Use *clud* and *clus* as clues to meaning when you come across words that contain this root.

When you see *clud* and *clus,* think of *se**clud**ed* (being "shut" away or "closed" off).

Clues to Meaning Use *clud* and *clus* as clues to the meanings of the underlined words.

Rather than enjoying her <u>inclusion</u> in the family, Annabelle chose to become a <u>recluse</u>. She lived her life alone—in <u>seclusion</u>, away from everyone else. When her sister and brother visited, she would <u>occlude</u> them—by refusing to unlock her door. Her family tried to figure out why she behaved this way, but their discussions were <u>inconclusive</u>. No one knew why or when she had started to act that way, but it seems safe to <u>conclude</u> that she isn't likely to change. Her cold behavior <u>precluded</u> family from visiting her. It was as if she lived in an <u>exclusive</u> club where no one was admitted except herself.

· ·

rid, ris | LIST 2

deride
derision
derisive
ridicule

Rid is a Latin root that means "laugh." Another way to spell this root is *ris*.

- Words containing *rid* or *ris* usually have something to do with laughter.

When you see *rid* and *ris,* think of *rid*iculous (something that is "laughable").

Clues to Meaning Use *rid* and *ris* as clues to the meanings of the underlined words.

Luis I know that Jayden's T-shirt looked weird, but I really don't like that so many people <u>ridiculed</u> him and laughed at his shirt. I don't like it when my friends <u>deride</u> others like that.

Ian Yeah, I thought the <u>derisive</u> laughter would never die down. Mocking laughter is one thing, but they just kept up the <u>derision</u>, teasing him all day.

· ·

In Your Notebook Write the list words and a sentence for each word in your notebook. Then draw a cartoon in which you use at least one of the words.

Figurative Language

Figurative language, such as idioms, can make reading and writing more interesting. An *idiom* is a commonly used phrase with a meaning that is different from the meaning of the words in the phrase. For example, saying that a job is "a piece of cake" doesn't make sense literally, but people understand it's a way of saying that a job is easy. Suppose someone says, "The concert, followed by two hours of karaoke, went *from the sublime to the ridiculous*." This idiom refers to going from something very good (the sublime) to something very silly (the ridiculous). Can you think of a few other idioms?

Apply and Extend

■ List 1

The word *conclude* is made from a Latin prefix (*con,* meaning "with") and a Latin root (*clud,* meaning "to close"). You *conclude* an essay by writing a *conclusion.* Write a sentence or two with both of these words, using context to show you understand the meanings.

■ List 1

Write a question about one of the words that contain *clud* or *clus.* The question should show that you understand the meaning of the word. For example, a question for the word *recluse* is: *What do you call a person who lives shut away or removed from the world?*

■ List 2

Think about how *ridiculous, deride,* and *derision* are related in meaning. Write a sentence with all three words. Use context to show you understand the meanings of the words.

Clue Review Play a word game with one of your classmates. Choose one of the list words. Give your partner a clue about the word. Did your partner guess the word correctly? If not, provide another clue until your partner correctly identifies the word. Then switch roles.

Did you know?
Occlusion can mean "being shut out." But when your dentist uses the word *occlusion,* he or she simply means the contact between your upper and lower teeth!

LIST WORDS

abode
abyss
bleak
diminutive
domicile
immensity
secluded
serene

Use Context as Clues to Meaning

Using vivid imagery when describing places helps to draw the reader into a story. When authors use precise words, their writing becomes much more exciting and interesting. What do you see in your mind as you read these two sentences? Which one describes more? Which one creates a stronger image in your mind?

> The hidden valley was very deep, with a river at the bottom.

> The surging river had carved a seemingly bottomless canyon, leaving a secluded wilderness behind.

The word *secluded* has the Latin root *clud,* which means "close" or "shut." A *secluded* place is one that is "closed off" or "shut away" from the world. Knowing the meaning of *secluded* helps you picture the scene that the author describes. *Secluded* also carries the connotation of peace and quiet.

Read this description. How does the context help you understand the meanings of the underlined words?

> She might have chosen anything from a penthouse to a mansion to a palace as her <u>abode</u>. However, the woman chose to live in a <u>diminutive</u> cottage by the sea. The tiny <u>domicile</u> had everything she wanted and needed in a home. Others may have seen its location as unwelcoming and lonely, but she did not see it as <u>bleak</u>. The woman loved the peaceful and <u>serene</u> spot, high atop a cliff overlooking the vast <u>immensity</u> of the ocean. She had chosen this <u>secluded</u> spot because its isolated location made visitors unlikely. Here, she could enjoy her days and nights shaping words into poems to portray the endless <u>abyss</u> of the sea and the unbroken blanket of the star-filled sky.

· ·

In Your Notebook After you read the description of the above scene, write the list words and their meanings. Then write three sentences using several of the list words to describe a *different* scene.

Using an Online Etymology Dictionary

The *etymology* of a word describes where the word came from and how its meaning has changed over time. For example, the root word of the noun *abode* is a mid-thirteenth-century Old English verb *abide,* meaning "to wait" or "remain behind." In the fifteenth century the word *abode* came to mean a person's home.

You can find similar facts and stories about other words in an online etymology dictionary, where you simply type in your word and hit "Enter" or "Search." The etymology of your word, as well as words with similar roots, will appear. As you read, notice how the meaning of the word has changed over time.

Apply and Extend

Have you heard these expressions?
- welcome to our humble abode
- into the abyss
- legal domicile

▢ Picture a favorite place. Use as many list words as you can to describe it. Use precise words so others can mentally picture it.

▢ The words *bleak, diminutive, secluded,* and *serene* carry connotations that help a writer create a mood. Select one of these list words and write one word that has a more positive connotation and one that has a more negative connotation.

Word History Select one of the list words that interests you. What can you find out about your word? Answer the following questions:

- From which language did your word originally come?

- What was the original meaning of the word?

- Has the meaning of the word changed over time?

- How does the modern meaning relate to the original one?

- What is one interesting fact you learned about the word?

LIST 1

consistent
persistent
resistance
restitution
station
stature
status
statute

sta, stit, sis

Sta is a Latin root that means "stand." Other spellings for this root are **stit** and **sis**.

When you see *sta, stit,* and *sis,* think of **sta**tue (a sculpture that is "standing").

Clues to Meaning Use *sta, stit,* and *sis* as clues to the meanings of the underlined words.

Ms. K It's good to see you, Mr. M. How's your restaurant doing?

Mr. M Better now! As you know, a local law didn't allow a restaurant to open across from a fire <u>station</u>. The concern was that restaurant traffic might interfere with the building. But we asked for a change in that <u>statute</u>, and it was granted.

Ms. K That's great! But, how did the firefighters react?

Mr. M Well, there was <u>resistance</u>. They were against the change. They thought we would keep them from doing their duty. So, we invited them for a free meal and talked about ways to control traffic.

Ms. K It pays to be <u>persistent</u>! You didn't give up, and now your restaurant is a success!

Mr. M Thanks! Working with the firefighters helped increase our <u>status</u> in town. A lot of people respected the way we handled that.

Ms. K And I hear the food and service are incredible!

Mr. M I try to give good, reliable, <u>consistent</u> service. If a customer has to wait longer than fifteen minutes for food, I make <u>restitution</u>—I make it up with a free meal.

Ms. K It's wonderful to see a new business owner of such great <u>stature</u> in this community. People really respect you!

LIST 2

capitalism
idealism
realism
terrorism

ism

Ism is a Greek suffix that means "condition" or "belief."

• To figure out words that end with the suffix *ism,* first identify the base word and then add *ism,* the suffix meaning "condition" or "belief."

When you see *ism,* think of *egotism* ("condition" of thinking, writing, or talking too much about oneself).

Clues to Meaning Use *ism* as a clue to the meanings of the underlined words.

- Under capitalism, individuals and groups of individuals own land, factories, and other means of production.

- Good partnerships often have two very different people. One might believe in idealism, following his or her dreams and ideals through life. A good partner for this person might be someone who believes in realism, or is practical and sees things as they really are.

- Individuals who believe in terrorism use violence, harming people and destroying property, to try to achieve their goals.

• •

In Your Notebook Write each list word and a time when you might encounter the word. For example, you might see the word *resistance* when you are studying the immune system in science class.

Using an Online Thesaurus

If you need a synonym or an antonym for a word such as *resistance*, you can use an online thesaurus. In an online thesaurus entry, you can expect to find information such as the word's part of speech, synonyms, and antonyms. Using a thesaurus can help you find precise, descriptive words to improve your writing.

To use an online thesaurus, type in the word and hit "enter" or "return" or "search."

- Read through the words the thesaurus lists as synonyms and antonyms.

- Choose the synonym or antonym that best expresses your intended meaning.

Apply and Extend

■ List 1

The words *consistent, persistent,* and *resistance* all come from the Latin *sistere,* which means "to stand." Write the prefix and its meaning for each word. For each word, what is "standing"? You may need to use a dictionary or an etymology dictionary.

■ List 1

The words *station, stature,* and *status* have several meanings. Look the words up in a dictionary. Then use each word in a sentence, demonstrating a different meaning than the one used in this lesson.

■ List 2

Choose one of the following words: *realism, capitalism, idealism,* or *terrorism.* Write a title for an article and include the word. Use context to show you understand the word's meaning. Then write a second title using another word from the list.

Act It Out Put your acting talent to work. Work with a partner to perform a skit based on the dialogue in this lesson. Become your character!

Did you know?
Other words with the root *sta* include *estate, stage, stance, stanza, state, statistic,* and *stay.*

bias
factual
generalization
hyperbole
jargon
omniscient
parentheses
repetitious

Use Context as Clues to Meaning

Mark Twain wrote during a time when authors filled their stories with accurate descriptions of life in America. This literary movement was called *realism*. Twain's novels were made-up stories, but he created realistic characters, dialogue, and settings.

While made-up stories can be realistic, they are not factual. The word *factual* means "concerned with fact," or "known to be true." *Fact* comes from the Latin *facere*, meaning "do." Factual information is used to report something that is true or that actually was done. At the right are more words related to language. You may come across them in your language arts class.

Read about ways that language is used. How does the context help you understand the meanings of the underlined words?

A reporter's job is to provide factual information, using only details that can be proved true. Sometimes a reporter allows his or her own bias, or personal feelings, into the writing. Then the writing is slanted toward one point of view.

Knowing certain uses of language will help you watch for bias. A generalization involves taking a particular fact or group of facts and making a broad, universal statement. For example, "All boys like to play baseball" is a generalization, and it is not true. Jargon can be words known only in one profession. For example, a science writer might use words like *nucleon* and *baryon* in a science article. Jargon can also be confused, meaningless talk or writing. Hyperbole is an intentional exaggeration, often silly or impossible, used for effect, such as, "I was trying to get here on time, but I ran into every red light in the state." A writer might repeat an idea over and over to emphasize it. This is a use of repetitious language. Writers may use another tool, parentheses, to set off words or phrases that are less important. Parentheses are curved lines that look like this: ( ).

Last, fiction writers can communicate their ideas by using an omniscient narrator in a story. Omniscient means "all-knowing," so the writer can have an all-knowing narrator report the characters' words and actions and also the writer's own feelings and thoughts.

• •

In Your Notebook Write each list word and provide an example. For example, for *bias*, you could write, "Men are always stronger than women."

Multiple Meanings

In sports, *bias* refers to a weight or a lop-sided edge of a ball that causes it to swerve. *Bias* comes from the Middle French word *biais* meaning "slant" or "oblique." Historically, it is associated with lawn bowling in France because the ball tended to roll in a curved course. One meaning of *bias* is "a slanting or diagonal line across a fabric." Another meaning is "prejudice, or a tendency to favor one side too much." If you think about it, these seemingly unlike meanings are not so dissimilar. A story or news account that is slanted shows bias by omitting or emphasizing certain facts.

Have you heard these words?

Gobbledygook = jargon that is wordy and hard to understand
Gibberish = jargon consisting of senseless chatter or nonsense talk

Apply and Extend

■ Some of the list words are unusual and unusual sounding. Choose two of your favorites from the eight words and use them in a sentence. Use context to show you understand the meaning of each word.

■ *Hyperboles* are common in everyday speech. Remember that they are impossible exaggerations. Work with a partner and list as many as you can. Share your list with another team.

Skit With a team of two or three classmates, create a skit with an *omniscient*, all-knowing narrator as one of the players. The others in the skit act and speak, and the narrator inserts comments about what they are feeling and thinking. The skit can be on any subject, but try to use examples of jargon, generalization, and/or bias to create humor. Have fun!

tang, tact LIST 1

LIST 1

intact
intangible
tact
tactful
tactile
tangent

Tang is a Latin root that means "touch." Another way to spell this root is *tact*.

- Use *tang* and *tact* as clues to meaning when you come across words that contain this root.
- When you see *tang* and *tact*, think of **tang**ible (capable of being "touched," material).

Clues to Meaning Use *tang* and *tact* as clues to the meanings of the underlined words.

- Ana was relieved to find the house <u>intact</u> after the tornado. The barn was gone, so how was the house undamaged?

- Although Alex liked holding the babysitting money he earned, he thought the <u>intangible</u> rewards of babysitting, especially the fun he had with the kids, were much more satisfying.

- Conner was not taking his sister to the concert. He knew he should be <u>tactful</u> and break the news to her gently. Unfortunately, he had no time and no <u>tact</u>, and he yelled at her on the way out the door.

- Sarah ran the velvet scarf through her hands, and its soft, <u>tactile</u> quality delighted her.

- For her birthday, Adele's father gave her a beautiful bracelet of <u>tangent</u> silver circles that barely seemed to touch each other.

fid LIST 2

LIST 2

confidant
confidential
diffident
fidelity
infidel
perfidy

Fid is a Latin root that means "trust."

- Words containing *fid* usually have something to do with trust or faithfulness.
- When you see *fid*, think of *con**fid**ence* ("trust" or faith in something or someone).

Clues to Meaning Use *fid* as a clue to the meanings of the underlined words.

Two weeks before, Lord Jaron had betrayed the trust of his best friend, Prince Rondile. Jaron had used secret information Rondile had told him in a plot against Rondile's father, the king. "Why would he commit such a perfidy?" cried Rondile. "He was my confidant, the one I told all my secrets to! And he exposed those confidential conversations!" Rondile worried that Jaron had pretended his fidelity all of these years. "He was never loyal to me. I thought he was a diffident, shy person, but now I find that he was sly and wicked. All he wanted was my father's throne. I should have known he was an infidel when he would not go to church with me anymore."

• •

In Your Notebook Write the list words. Then choose two words and make a 4-square concept map for each word.

Literary Allusions

Fidelity, or the absence of it, recurs over and over again as a theme in literature throughout the ages. For example, in Shakespeare's play *Julius Caesar*, Brutus takes part in the Roman emperor's assassination. As Brutus draws his knife, Caesar expresses his surprise and sadness at his best friend's infidelity, crying out, "Et tu, Brute?" The question, which means, "And you also, Brutus?" has come to express the pain one feels at betrayal by a confidant.

Apply and Extend

■ List 1

The word *tactic* looks like it might share a root with these list words. Research the origin of *tactic* and compare its root to the list words formed from the *tact* root. Write a sentence or two explaining the difference in meaning between these two words drawn from *tact*.

■ List 2

Write a question about one of the words in List 2, showing that you understand the meaning of the word. An example question for the word *infidel* is: *Which word describes someone who doesn't believe in religion?*

■ List 2

Write one sentence using as many of the list words as you can. Challenge yourself. Can you use all six words in one sentence?

Word Part Invention How much of a wordsmith are you? With a partner, combine word parts from this lesson with other letters or syllables to invent a new word. Then write a definition for the word based on the meanings of the word parts. Share the word and definition with classmates.

Have you heard these expressions?
- to go off on a tangent
- *Semper Fidelis*
- bona fide

LIST WORDS

core
crust
lava
magma
mantle
molten
plate
prime

Use Context as Clues to Meaning

The material that Earth is made of is tactile: you can pick up soil and rock and touch it and run it through your fingers. The study of the Earth and what it is made of is called *geology*. The word *geology* has two parts. *Geo* is a Greek root meaning "Earth," and *ology* comes from the Greek for "science of." At the left are more words related to geology. You may come across these words in your science class.

Read more about geology. How does the context help you understand the meanings of the underlined words?

The Earth is a busy place, inside and out. Between its outer <u>crust</u> (the outer layer) and the <u>core</u> at its very center, geological forces and extreme heat are at work in a layer called the <u>mantle</u>—melting, moving, and molding <u>magma</u>. This liquefied rock circulates around the <u>mantle</u> until it is forced up and out as <u>lava</u> from volcanoes. Huge rock pieces called <u>plates</u> float atop the <u>molten</u> or liquefied material in the <u>mantle</u>. The continents ride on these <u>plates</u>, moving slowly around the Earth's surface in a slow geological dance called continental drift. The movement of these plates is the <u>prime</u>—the most important—reason for certain types of earthquakes.

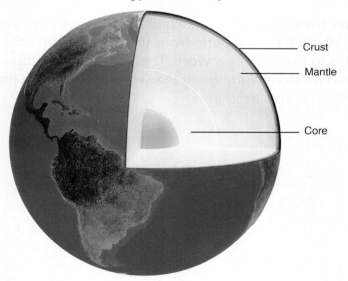

Crust

Mantle

Core

In Your Notebook Write the list words and their meanings. Then draw and label a diagram of the Earth's layers.

Using a Glossary

Each branch of the sciences has its own special vocabulary; sometimes it seems like learning a different language. Many science books help readers by providing a glossary of specialized words related to a particular science. A *glossary* (literally, "a place for a different tongue") lists special words alphabetically and gives their definitions. To find the glossary, look in the back of the book. In addition to definitions, glossaries often provide the pronunciations and parts of speech for words. Next time you are reading a science book, check the glossary to find the meanings of words you don't know.

Apply and Extend

Have you heard these terms?
- lava lamp
- prime suspect

■ Many of the list words have a meaning other than their scientific meaning. For example, a plate is a large mass of rock, but it is also what your food is placed on. Write a sentence each for as many of the list words as you can with context that tells their other meanings.

■ The word *mantle* can also mean a "cloak," or can be a verb meaning "to cover." In fact, *mantle* comes from the Latin for "cloak." Write one or two sentences about why you think scientists use this word to describe the band of molten rock that surrounds the Earth's core.

Clue Review Play a word game with one of your classmates. Choose one of the list words. Give your partner a clue about the word. Did your partner guess the word correctly? If not, provide another clue until your partner correctly identifies the word. Then switch roles.

LESSON 37 Word Parts and Meanings
lit, plex, pli, ply

LIST 1

literacy
literary
literate
obliterate

lit

Lit is a Latin root that means "writing" or "letter."

- Words containing *lit* usually have something to do with letters, writing, or reading.
- Use *lit* as a clue to meaning when you come across words that contain this root.
- When you see *lit,* think of **lit**erature (the "writings" of a period, language, or country).

Clues to Meaning Use *lit* as a clue to the meanings of the underlined words.

- Now that more schools have begun to emphasize reading and writing in the curriculum, students' <u>literacy</u> is at an all-time high.

- I like all of your references to other writers and poets in your research paper. I think it makes you sound <u>literary</u>.

- I suggest you ask the students who are computer <u>literate</u> and know how to use them to help those students who do not yet understand the new software.

- She knew that if she pressed the Delete key, she would <u>obliterate</u> what she had typed and might not be able to get it back.

• •

LIST 2

complex
complexion
complicate
comply
imply
perplexed
pliant
supplication

plex, pli, ply

Plex is a Latin root that means "fold" or "twine." Other ways to spell this root are *pli* and *ply*.

- Words containing this root usually have something to do with things that are folded or entwined, either literally or figuratively.
- Use *plex, pli,* and *ply* as clues to meaning when you come across words that contain this root.
- When you see *plex, pli,* and *ply,* think of *du***plex** ("twofold," or having two parts).

Clues to Meaning Use *plex, pli,* and *ply* as clues to the meanings of the underlined words.

My friend Zoe is <u>complicated</u>. You never know what she's thinking. I don't mean to <u>imply</u> that there's anything bad about her; I would never suggest that. But here's an example: Last night, she studied her face in the mirror for an hour. Her <u>complexion</u> is beautiful— her soft, <u>pliant</u> skin was spotless. But she was sure she saw a pimple. That left me feeling confused and <u>perplexed</u>. She begged me to go to the store and buy her some face cream. She was so desperate, she got on her knees in <u>supplication</u>. I was afraid that if I didn't <u>comply</u>, I wouldn't have anyone to hang out with that night. So I went to the store. When I got back, we tried to read the <u>complex</u> instructions for using the cream. There were so many steps that we couldn't figure out how to use it. Suddenly, Zoe decided that her face was fine. No cream needed. See what I mean? <u>Complicated</u>!

. . . .

In Your Notebook Write each list word, along with a synonym or meaning for it. Check your work in a dictionary.

Antonym Study

An antonym is a word with a meaning that is opposite of another word's meaning. Sometimes adding a prefix changes a word into an antonym, as in *illiterate, illiteracy, nonliterary,* and *uncomplicated*. In other cases, an antonym is an entirely different word. Some antonyms for *complex* are *simple, uncomplicated,* and *straightforward*. Check a thesaurus for antonyms for specific words.

■ List 1

Look up the word *obliterate* in a dictionary. How is the word related to the *lit* root? Write a sentence describing what you found.

■ List 2

Look up the meaning and etymology of *supplication*. What physical action is the word related to, and how does the action relate to the word's meaning? Write one or two sentences using the word.

■ List 2

Use what you know about prefixes and suffixes to infer the meanings of the following words: *complexity, complication, complicated, implication, implicated, perplexity*. Choose three of the words and try writing a sentence using all three correctly.

Clue Review Play a word game with one of your classmates. Choose one of the list words. Give your partner a clue about the word. Did your partner guess the word correctly? If not, provide another clue until your partner correctly identifies the word. Then switch roles.

Have you heard these expressions?
- literary giant
- literary masterpiece

boundary
isthmus
landform
landmark
latitude
longitude
peninsula
prairie

Use Context as Clues to Meaning

Geography is the study of Earth's surface and its features, both natural and man-made. Two tools used in locating Earth's features are longitude and latitude. *Longitude* comes from the Latin word *longitudo* and means "length," while *latitude* comes from the Latin word *latitudo* and means "width." Mapmakers have created north-south lines of longitude and east-west circles of latitude that cover the globe and help us find specific locations. At the right are more words related to geography. You may come across these words in your social studies class.

Read about the state of Wisconsin. What context clues help you understand the meanings of the underlined words?

The state of Wisconsin is bordered by Lake Michigan on the east and the state of Michigan and Lake Superior on the north. The south and southwest borders of the state closely follow the <u>boundary</u>, or border, between the tallgrass <u>prairie</u> land of Iowa and northern Illinois and the forest land that reaches northward into Canada. Wisconsin has a large <u>peninsula</u>, a piece of land almost completely surrounded by water, jutting northeast into Lake Michigan. Another major <u>landform</u>, or land feature, is the famous Wisconsin Dells, a gorge formed by glaciers long ago. The state capital, Madison, is located on an <u>isthmus</u>—a narrow strip of land—between Lake Mendota and Lake Monona. To find Madison on a globe, look where these two lines cross: <u>latitude</u> 43° 07' North (horizontal line north of the equator) and <u>longitude</u> 89° 40' West (north-south line that is west of the 0° line). The best-known <u>landmark</u>, or well-known location, in Madison is the Capitol Building, which sits in the center of the city.

• •

In Your Notebook Write the list words. Then create a sketch illustrating each word.

Multiple Meanings

Notice how the word *latitude* is used in this sentence.

The artists who lived in the warmer <u>latitudes</u> of the Mediterranean enjoyed much <u>latitude</u> in creating amazing pieces of art.

The word *latitude* comes from a Latin word that means "wide." Roman maps were much wider than they were long, and lines of latitude went across the wide way. In geography, *latitude* means "a distance north or south of the equator," but *latitude* can also refer to a feeling of freedom from rules that are narrow, which is the opposite of wide.

Did you know?

Many place-names in the United States come from Native American words and names. However, Native American languages do not share roots with English words.

Apply and Extend

■ Identify three additional landforms, give their names, and explain what they are.

■ Identify the following in the city, area, or state in which you live: a landform, a landmark, and a boundary.

Graphic Gallery Use your skills as a cartoonist to create a comic strip about the first explorers or settlers to arrive in your area using words from this lesson. Draw pictures and write dialogue or use an online program to create the graphic text. How many of the words can you use? Compile the class's comic strips into a Graphic Gallery.

sent, sens   LIST 1

Sent is a Latin root that means "to feel." Another way to spell this root is *sens*.

- Words containing *sent* or *sens* usually have something to do with some type of feeling.
- Use *sent* and *sens* as clues to meaning when you come across words that contain this root.

When you see *sent* and *sens*, think of **sent**iment (sincere "feelings").

assent
consent
dissent
resent
sensation
sensory
sensuous
sentient

Clues to Meaning Use *sent* and *sens* as clues to the meanings of the underlined words.

- I know my dog is <u>sentient</u> because he is aware of everything that goes on around him. He also knows what I am feeling because he snuggles up next to me when I'm sad. Petting him is a <u>sensory</u> treat. The softness of his fur under my fingers is one of my favorite <u>sensations</u>, or feelings. It's such a <u>sensuous</u>, pleasurable feeling that it makes me forget what I'm worried about.

- I think I will <u>assent</u> to your request and say yes. I will give you my <u>consent</u>, or permission, to borrow my bike for the day. I know you would <u>resent</u> it and be unhappy if I said no. I don't like the way you talk to me when we <u>dissent</u>, even though a little disagreement between two people is normal.

. . . .

val   LIST 2

Val is a Latin root that means "strong."

- Words containing *val* usually have something to do with having strength or worth.

When you see *val*, think of **val**iant (having or showing "strength," such as courage or bravery).

ambivalent
convalescent
evaluation
invalid

Clues to Meaning Use *val* as a clue to the meanings of the underlined words.

After her examination of the patient, the doctor shared her <u>evaluation</u> of the man's condition. In her opinion, an accident like his might make some people an <u>invalid</u>—weak and unable to get out of bed for months. But this patient is healthier than most and is not <u>ambivalent</u> about getting better; he shows no conflicting feelings. Instead, he is so determined to get better that I'm sure he will need only a very short <u>convalescent</u> period to recover before he's back to his full strength.

• •

In Your Notebook As you read the clues to meaning, write the list words and their meanings in your notebook. If you're not sure of the meanings, check them in a dictionary.

Dictionary Pronunciations

Look up the word *invalid* in the dictionary. Notice that there are two entries, separated into different syllables. The word *in' va lid* may be a noun or an adjective. The word *in val' id* is an adjective. An accent mark is a diagonal line placed to the upper right of a syllable. It means that you should emphasize that part of the word when you speak. For example, one pronunciation for *invalid* emphasizes the first syllable, while another emphasizes the second syllable. Use the dictionary to help with pronunciations and to compare and contrast word meanings.

Apply and Extend

■ List 1

The words *consent* and *dissent* can be used as both nouns and verbs. Choose one of the words. Write a sentence using the word as both a noun and a verb.

■ List 1

How are the words *assent, resent, dissent,* and *consent* related to "feeling"? How does each of the four prefixes added to the root word *sent* change the root's meaning? If you wish, check the meanings of the prefixes in a dictionary or online.

■ List 2

Work with a partner. Choose a word and write a "What if" question, such as *What if someone is convalescent?* Answer each other's question. An answer to this question might be *The person needs to rest to continue to recover.*

The Illustrated Word Sharpen your pencils—it's time to play a picture game. Divide a group into two teams. Write lesson words on cards and place them in a stack upside down. The first person on Team 1 takes a card, draws a picture that represents the word on the card, and shows the picture to his or her team. If team members guess the word in 30 seconds, the team gets a point. Now it's Team 2's turn.

Have you heard these expressions?
- an invalid argument
- sensory overload
- parental consent

Use Context as Clues to Meaning

The word *expression* comes from several Latin word parts that originally meant "to press or squeeze out." Even if people don't "squeeze out" tears, the *expressions* on their faces often tell you what sensations, or feelings, they are experiencing. In math, the word *expression* has a different meaning. Can you "squeeze out" what *expression* means based on the following examples?

$$3 + x \qquad 12 \div 4 \qquad 2a \times 3b$$

If you said that an *expression* is a group of numbers, letters, and operators (+, −, ×, ÷) that show a mathematical operation or quantity, you are correct! The words in this list are all related to math, so you may come across them in your math class.

Read this passage from a math book. How does the context help you understand the meanings of the underlined words?

In a simple <u>expression</u>, or mathematical statement, changing the order of the addends does not change the value. For example, $3 + x$ equals $x + 3$. The same property applies to simple <u>expressions</u> with multiplication. So, $5 \times y$ equals $y \times 5$. There is no <u>probability</u>, or chance, that the expressions are not equal.

Now, let's look at an equation: $3 \times x = y$. In this equation, we have two unknown values: x and y. The values of x and y can change, or vary, so each letter is called a <u>variable</u>. The first, x, is an <u>independent variable</u> because you can choose any value for x without worrying about other variables in the equation. The value of y "depends on" the value of x. Therefore, y is called a <u>dependent variable</u>.

The <u>domain</u> for this equation includes all possible values of the independent variable x. The <u>range</u> includes all possible values of the dependent variable y. The equation $3 \times x = y$ is like a number machine. The operation you do on x in order to get y and the number you use in the operation make up the <u>function</u> of the machine. For this equation, the function is "multiply x by 3."

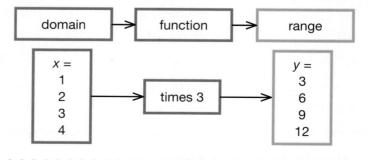

In Your Notebook Write the list words and their meanings. Use several of the words in a sentence or two to describe a math problem.

Context Clues

The context, or words around an unfamiliar word, often help you figure out the meaning of that word. Watch for definitions, synonyms, antonyms, examples, or descriptions that offer clues to the unfamiliar word. For example, the sentence *The values of x and y can change, or vary, so each letter is called a variable* tells you that *vary* means "to change." You can use the clue to figure out that a *variable* is a value that can change. The diagram on the previous page shows you examples of *domain, function,* and *range* to help you figure out what each word means.

> **Did you know?**
> The word *function* comes from a Latin word meaning "to perform." A math function describes how to "perform" the operations shown in the expression.

Apply and Extend

▪ The word *dependent* comes from a Latin word meaning "to hang down." This meaning was later broadened to mean "to be attached to." In math, the value of the dependent variable is "attached to" the value of the independent variable. Write two or three sentences telling how *independent* relates to *dependent*.

▪ The word *range* has general meanings beyond its meaning in math. Write two sentences, each using a different meaning of *range*. Use context to show you understand both meanings.

Word History Choose an interesting word from this week's lesson. What can you find out about the history and origins of your word? Answer the following questions:

- From which language did your word derive?
- What is the first recorded instance of its use in the English language?
- What is one interesting fact you learned about the word?
- List related words that you find.

LIST 1

launder
lavatory
lavish

lau, lav

Lau is a Latin root that means "wash." Another way to spell this root is *lav*.

ANCHOR WORD
laundry

- Words containing *lau* or *lav* usually have something to do with washing.
- When you see *lau* and *lav*, think of *laundry* (clothes, towels, and bedding to be "washed").

Clues to Meaning Use *lau* and *lav* as clues to the meanings of the underlined words.

- **Luz** I need to wash up after the long flight. Where is the lavatory?

- **Kylie** The bathroom is just down the hall. I'm so glad you're here. I've planned a feast for tonight. It will be a lavish meal!

- **Luz** Sounds great! I have dirty clothes to launder. I hope I have time to wash them before the guests arrive.

LIST 2

ablution
antediluvian
deluge
dilution

lu

Lu is a Latin root that means "wash."

ANCHOR WORD
dilu**te**

- Words containing *lu* usually have something to do with washing.
- When you see *lu*, think of *dilute* (make weaker or thinner by "washing" or flooding it with water).

Clues to Meaning Use *lu* as a clue to the meanings of the underlined words.

My grandmother always says, "I've finished my ablutions," meaning she has washed up. I tell her that *ablution* is an antediluvian word. It's so old-fashioned that no one uses it anymore!

We had a heavy rainstorm. Gran called it a deluge. To warm us up, she made a pot of hot tea. Afterward, she thought the tea was too hot and needed dilution. She added cold water to the tea, but the water made it weaker.

flu

affluence
confluence
fluctuate
fluent
influence

Flu is a Latin root that means "flow."

ANCHOR WORD
fluid

- Use *flu* as a clue to meaning when you come across words that contain this root.
- When you see *flu,* think of **flu**id (any substance that "flows").

Clues to Meaning Use *flu* as a clue to the meanings of the underlined words.

Jack Mr. Chan was born in China, but he is <u>fluent</u> in English. He speaks it so easily that the words just flow! He grew up near the <u>confluence</u> of two rivers, where the rivers flow together. The <u>affluence</u> here amazes him since everyone seems to be wealthy.

Campbell Mr. Chan is a positive <u>influence</u>. Interesting ideas just flow from him to his students. He makes learning about the stock market fun. He explained how the market <u>fluctuates</u> all day; the stocks' values change, moving up and down as they're bought and sold.

• •

In Your Notebook Write all of the list words and their meanings.

Biblical Allusions

An implied or indirect reference in literature or in speech is an allusion. Allusions to events and people in Bible stories are common. For example, in one story, God told Noah to make an ark to save his family, himself, and a pair of each kind of animal from the coming flood. Today a reference to "building an ark" or "Noah's ark" is an allusion to preparing for a *deluge*—a heavy rain—or a flood.

Apply and Extend

■ List 1

Write one sentence using as many of the list words as you can. Challenge yourself. Can you use all three words in one sentence?

■ List 2

The word *deluge* comes from the prefix *dis,* meaning "away" and the root *luere,* meaning "to wash." Usually a *deluge* is a heavy rainfall, but it can refer to anything that overwhelms, such as homework. Write a sentence or two using *deluge* with reference to something other than rain.

■ List 3

The word *influence* can be used as both a noun and a verb. Write one sentence using the noun form and one using the verb form. Include context to show you understand the meaning of the word. Show your sentences to a partner. Have your partner identify how you used *influence* in each sentence.

Act It Out Put your acting talent to work. Work with a partner to perform a skit based on one of the passages in this lesson. Become your character!

LIST WORDS

decadent
desolate
eloquent
emphatic
quaint
sinister
stealthy
superficial

Use Context as Clues to Meaning

Words in literary descriptions help readers visualize scenes, characters, and actions. Writers use description to add vivid, colorful details to paint pictures in words. Suppose you want to describe a character's changing moods. If you write that the character's mood *fluctuates,* you indicate that it continually rises and falls. *Fluctuates* comes from the Latin root *flu,* which means "to flow." A fluctuating mood is constantly "flowing," or moving in waves. If you use the word *fluctuates,* you are painting a more colorful picture than if you use the word *changes.*

Read this discussion, which takes place in a language arts class. How does the context help you understand the meanings of the underlined words?

Gianna loved the mystery story. She said, "The author uses the word <u>quaint</u> to describe the setting. That word helps me picture a pleasant, old-fashioned village."

Olivia said that early on, the writer hints that evil is lurking. She quoted from the story, "On the surface, everything in Spring Town seems normal—all cozy homes and well-kept lawns—but behind that <u>superficial</u> appearance, a <u>sinister</u> plot threatens to destroy the calm."

Marshall added, "Rochester, the villain, grew up in a house outside the village on a barren piece of land. The author writes that no trees, flowers, or curtains on the windows soften the <u>desolate</u>, lonely look of that house. The <u>decadent</u> property has been in decline for years. Everything shows decay, from a broken window to the sunken walk."

Gianna added, "In the beginning, the author describes Rochester as an <u>eloquent</u> young man who speaks with ease. His voice is <u>emphatic</u>, strong, and forceful. Yet in the end his purpose is to gain power over others. In reality, he is sneaky and sly, and he <u>stealthily</u> tries to draw others into his evil plan."

• •

In Your Notebook Write each list word. Next to it, write a word for someone, some place, or something it might describe.

Connotation and Denotation

A word's connotation is what is suggested beyond the literal, exact meaning. Its denotation is the literal meaning. For example, the denotation of *decadent* is "growing worse" or "declining." The connotations are unfavorable because *decadent* can mean "decaying," "immoral," or "corrupt." The dictionary meaning of *eloquent* is "very expressive." This word has favorable connotations and means "graceful" or "well-spoken." You can rank words that have similar but slightly different meanings from having a neutral connotation to having the most negative or most positive connotation. For example, in this group of words—*bad, harmful, sinister*—*sinister* has the most negative connotation.

Have you heard these expressions?

- a stealth bomber
- a stealth virus
- a stealth candidate

Apply and Extend

■ Write *quaint* and its dictionary definition. Then write three words that have meanings similar to *quaint* and put them in order from the one with the most neutral connotation to the one with the most positive connotation.

■ *Eloquent, sinister, stealthy,* and *superficial* are adjectives that can be used to describe individuals. For each word, make up a character and write a sentence that conveys something about how he or she acts.

Act It Out Put your acting talent to work. Work with several classmates to perform a skit based on the passage in this lesson. Choose a narrator and students to play the characters in the passage. Become your character!

junct   LIST 1

adjunct
injunction
junction
juncture

Junct is a Latin root that means "join."

- Words containing *junct* usually have something to do with joining two things.
- When you see *junct,* think of *con**junct**ion* (a "joining" together).

Clues to Meaning Use *junct* as a clue to the meanings of the underlined words.

- Trey stopped to rest at the <u>junction</u> of the two rivers. At this place where the rivers joined, he could see many miles down both waterways.

- After their argument, Megan and Annie were facing a <u>juncture</u> in their friendship. They had to decide if their disagreement would break them apart.

- Sam's mom issued an <u>injunction</u> against computer games, commanding Sam not to play until his homework was done.

- "He makes me feel like his <u>adjunct</u>," Carlotta complained about her brother to Gwennie. "But I am not his assistant!"

- -

tain, ten   LIST 2

appertain
detain
maintain
pertain
tenacious
tenant
tendentious
untenable

Tain is a Latin root that means "contain" or "hold." Another way to spell this root is *ten.*

- Words containing *tain* or *ten* usually have something to do with holding or containing.
- The word *contain* has a Latin prefix and a Latin root.

con (together) + tain (hold) = contain

When you see *tain* and *ten,* think of *con**tain*** ("hold" or have within itself).

Clues to Meaning Use *tain* and *ten* as clues to the meanings of the underlined words.

"Your position is untenable. You can't defend it!" growled Sir Gren. "Why do you insist on making such a tendentious, one-sided argument? There are other sides to this issue."

But Fanule was tenacious and would not let go of the argument. "Your knights have no right to detain my son. They put him in prison for taking a pig!"

Sir Gren retorted, "Your son is charged with theft, which pertains to his taking a pig that belonged to me. That is a crime."

"Without him, I can't maintain your land. I just can't keep up with the work!" responded Fanule. "We may be mere tenant farmers, renting but not owning your land, Sir, but you need us to work the land. Our work appertains to a healthy harvest for all of your people."

• •

In Your Notebook Write the list words. Then choose two words and make a 4-square concept map for each word.

Analogy Study

An analogy is a comparison between two pairs of words. The words in each pair are related in the same way. For example, they can be synonyms, such as *pertain* and *appertain*. An analogy with these list words is *Pertain is to appertain as entertain is to amuse.*

Analogies can also show other types of relationships, such as the following:

Antonyms: *Detain is to release as admire is to disdain.*

Description: *Tenacious is to lawyer as tendentious is to politician.*

Task: *Injunction is to judge as blueprint is to architect.*

Apply and Extend

■ List 1

Write a question about one of the words that contains *junct,* showing that you understand the meaning of the word. An example question for the word *adjunct* is: *Which word is something connected with a more important thing?*

■ List 2

Choose four of the list words. Each has *tain* or *ten.* What does each word have to do with containing or holding? In other words, what is being contained or held?

■ List 2

Don't confuse the words *tenet* and *tenant.* Though they come from the same root, they have very different meanings. Research these two words to find how they are related, and explain their differences in two or three sentences.

Rap It Up Working with a classmate, choose a word from this lesson and use the word and its definition correctly in a rap or poem such as the following. Compile your rap with other classmates' raps into a Rap It Up notebook.

> My little brother won't go to sleep!
> He keeps tossing pillows at my tired feet.
> "Stop being so tenacious!" I shout.
> But he's too young to know what I'm talking about.
> "It means 'not giving up,'" I explain.
> But my attempt to teach him is in vain.
> I'm covered in pillows, and he's wide awake.
> I'm not sure how many more nights I can take.
> I wish my brother was a lot less tenacious
> and our camping tent a lot more spacious!

> **Did you know?**
> The word *lieutenant* combines the French word *place (lieu)* and the English word *tenant,* meaning "holder." A lieutenant can act in place of someone in higher authority.

LIST WORDS

memoir
misconstrue
observation
realistic
revision
sarcasm
translation
transpose

Use Context as Clues to Meaning

Both rich and famous people as well as ordinary people have a great curiosity about other people's lives. It is not surprising, therefore, that when a well-known person writes a *memoir,* the story of the person's life and thoughts, it generally will become a bestselling book. At the left are words related to writing that you might come across in memoirs and other books and articles. You may also read these words in your language arts class.

Read about some words related to writing. How does the context help you understand the meanings of the underlined words?

• People write <u>memoirs</u> to record their memories and their personal <u>observations</u>, their thoughts about their lives. Anyone reading a <u>memoir</u> can have a <u>realistic</u> look into the writer's life, seeing what actually happened.

• "Why don't we let Miss Know-It-All tell us all about it?" mocked Jen with <u>sarcasm</u>. Sara was hurt by Jen making fun of her.

• Type *form* and *from*. If you <u>transpose</u>, or switch, the letters *o* and *r,* your computer's spellcheck program will not pick up the mistake.

• Leon was afraid his readers might <u>misconstrue</u> his story as pertaining to politics, and he wanted them to understand what he was saying. He decided to make some <u>revisions</u> to his story, and he changed some key sentences to make his message clearer.

• Most people can't read the original Hebrew Bible, so they purchase a <u>translation</u> written in English or another language they can read.

• •

In Your Notebook Write each list word and its meaning. If you need to check a meaning, use a dictionary.

Puns

Playing with words can be fun. Can you think of a funny way to use a word so that it has more than one meaning? This kind of play on words is called a *pun*. Benjamin Franklin used a pun as he signed the Declaration of Independence: "We must all hang together, or assuredly we shall all hang separately." Franklin was warning the signers to be loyal to one another because the English government could arrest and hang them all as traitors.

Authors of memoirs love to use puns as titles. Comedian Jerry Seinfeld wrote an autobiography called *Sein Language,* a play on his last name. Roger Moore, famous for playing James Bond in movies, titled his memoir *My Word Is My Bond*. Puns make good jokes:

Why did the pony go to the doctor? Because she was a little horse (hoarse).

Why can a man never starve in the desert? Because he can eat the sand which is there. (sandwiches there)

Did you know?
Although the origin of the word *pun* is a mystery, it may come from the same Latin root for "point" as the word *punctuation*.

Apply and Extend

◼ Two of the list words include the prefix *trans,* a Latin prefix meaning "across." What is "going across" what in each case?

◼ Imagine you are writing your memoir. Which four list words might you be able to use in your memoir? Why?

Clue Review Play a word game with one of your classmates. Choose one of the list words. Give your partner a clue about the word. Did your partner guess the word correctly? If not, provide another clue until your partner correctly identifies the word. Then switch roles.

LIST 1

conspire
expire
inspire
perspiration
spirit
transpire

spir

re**spir**ation

Spir is a Latin root that means "breathe."

- Words containing *spir* usually have something to do with breathing.
- When you see *spir,* think of *respiration* ("breathing").

Clues to Meaning Use *spir* as a clue to the meanings of the underlined words.

- I saw my former "friends" in the cafeteria whispering, but they stopped when they saw me. They must be meeting to <u>conspire</u> against me—I bet they're plotting to embarrass me.

- Hey, this free movie pass is going to <u>expire</u> on Monday. We'd better use it this weekend, because it won't be good after that.

- People who have overcome difficulties <u>inspire</u> me. They make me want to rise above my problems and be a better, happier person.

- He had a problem with <u>perspiration</u> during public speaking. He would get so nervous that he would sweat through his shirt.

- Come to the game on Saturday and show some school <u>spirit</u>! Get excited and cheer on our team!

- I knew something bad would <u>transpire</u> while I was out of the room. A big argument broke out after I left.

· ·

LIST 2

aerate
aerial
aerodynamic
aeronautics
aerosol
aerospace

aer

aerobics

Aer is a Greek root that means "air."

- Words containing *aer* usually have something to do with the air or the atmosphere.
- Use *aer* as a clue to meaning when you come across words that contain this root.
- When you see *aer,* think of *aerobics* (exercise that gets you breathing a lot of "air").

Clues to Meaning Use *aer* as a clue to the meanings of the underlined words.

- You have to <u>aerate</u> the water in a fish tank. Bubbles from the pump dissolve oxygen, a gas that fish need to survive, into the water.

- In addition to large attacks by land and by sea, invaders launched an <u>aerial</u> attack with thirty fighter jets.

- The <u>aerodynamic</u> features of jets, their sleek smoothness, help them deal with air pressure and other gases in the atmosphere, and help them fly better.

- All I ever wanted to do was study <u>aeronautics</u>. I wanted to learn about the physics of flight, aircraft construction, and the Federal Aviation Authority. And, of course, I wanted to learn to fly.

- To use an <u>aerosol</u> air freshener, push a button at the top of the can, and the air pressure in the can releases a mist into the air.

- To get to space, you have to travel through Earth's atmosphere, so <u>aerospace</u> engineers study both flight in air and flight in space.

· ·

In Your Notebook Write each list word and its meaning. If possible, use an illustration to define the word.

Connotation and Denotation

Synonyms are words with similar meanings. However, their precise meanings and connotations may differ. A word's connotation is what is suggested beyond the word's denotation, or literal meaning. For example, synonyms for *conspire* include *scheme,* which has a negative connotation, and *collaborate,* which has a positive connotation.

You can rank synonyms on a continuum from having negative connotations to neutral to positive connotations.

scheme	collude	conspire	associate	collaborate
negative		**neutral**		**positive**

119

Apply and Extend

■ List 1

The word *expire* has several meanings. Write two sentences, each using a different meaning of *expire*. Use context to show you understand both meanings.

■ List 1

Perspiration is a noun made from a verb; the final *e* on the verb was changed to *a* and the suffix *tion* was added. *Expire* and *inspire* are verbs that can be turned into nouns using this same process. Choose one of these words. Write one sentence using the noun form and one sentence using the verb form.

■ List 2

Write a question about one of the words on List 2, showing that you understand the meaning of the word. An example question for the word *aerate* is: *Which word means "to fill with a gas"?*

Word Part Invention How much of a wordsmith are you? With a partner, combine word parts from this lesson with other letters or syllables to invent a new word. Then write a definition for the word based on the meanings of the word parts. Share the word and definition with classmates.

Do you know these expressions?
- She helped in a spirit of kindness.
- The judge upheld the spirit of the law.

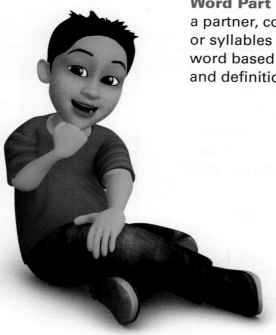

120

LIST WORDS

carnivore
compete
herbivore
niche
omnivore
predator
scavenger
symbiotic

Use Context as Clues to Meaning

An ecosystem is an environment in which living organisms try to find the things they need to stay alive. Ponds, meadows, and forests are ecosystems.

At the right are some words related to ecosystems. You may come across these words in your science class.

Read the paragraphs below. How does the context help you understand the meanings of the underlined words?

Each organism in an ecosystem occupies a <u>niche</u> and has its own role in a food web. For example, an <u>herbivore</u>, such as a rabbit, eats mainly plants. A <u>carnivore</u>, or meat eater, such as a hawk, eats mainly animals. An <u>omnivore</u>, such as a mouse, eats both plants and animals.

To survive, an animal <u>competes</u> for food, or tries to get the food before others do. Another threat to survival is <u>predators</u>, which prey on other animals. <u>Scavengers</u> eat only dead animals.

In a <u>symbiotic</u> relationship, two unlike living things benefit from living together. Have you ever seen lichen growing on the side of a tree? Lichens are fungi and algae living together. The fungi provide shelter, and the algae provide food. Together, it's room and board!

• •

In Your Notebook Write the list words. Then choose three or four of those words and write a few sentences explaining how the words are related.

Context Clues

Use context clues—the words or sentences around a word—to figure out the meaning of an unfamiliar word. For example, words and phrases such as *although, on the other hand,* and *while* signal that two words have contrasting meanings. In the sentence that follows, the word *while* indicates a contrast.

> *While a <u>predator</u> hunts to get food, a <u>scavenger</u> eats only animals that are already dead or have been left by hunters.*

This sentence shows how predators and scavengers are different: scavengers do not hunt to get food.

Did you know?

Many scientific terms are special uses of words you hear in daily life. Teams *compete* for a trophy, people go on *scavenger* hunts, and students try to find their *niche* in life.

Apply and Extend

■ The word *niche* has multiple meanings, one of which is science related as taught in this lesson. Do you know any general, or common, meanings for *niche?* If not, you can consult a dictionary. Write three sentences using *niche.* One sentence should reflect its science-related meaning; two sentences should reflect its other general meanings.

■ What common root do the words *carnivore, herbivore,* and *omnivore* have? Use an online dictionary to find the meaning of this root. Then write a sentence using the three words in context.

Clue Review Play a word game with one of your classmates. Choose one of the list words. Give your partner a clue about the word. For example, for the word *carnivore,* you might pretend to eat a chicken leg. Did your partner guess the word correctly? If not, provide another clue until your partner correctly identifies the word. Then switch roles.

pel, puls

LIST 1

compel
compulsory
dispel
expulsion
impulse
propel
pulsate
repulsive

Pel is a Latin root that means "drive" or "push." Another way to spell this root is *puls*.

- Words containing *pel* or *puls* usually have to do with feeling driven or pushing to do something.
- Use *pel* and *puls* as clues to meaning when you come across words that contain this root.

  (ANCHOR WORD) **expel** When you see *pel* or *puls,* think of ex**pel** (to "drive" out with force).

Clues to Meaning Use *pel* and *puls* as clues to the meanings of the underlined words.

- High school classes in English, math, and science are <u>compulsory</u> courses, which means everyone has to take them. Failure to take them could lead to <u>expulsion</u> from school. And if you are expelled, you won't have the diploma you need to go to college or find a good job.

- I wanted to <u>dispel</u> my friend's gloomy mood after she lost her tennis game. To drive away her sadness, I dragged her to the school dance. When we got there, my favorite song started playing. Suddenly I had an <u>impulse</u> to grab my friend's hand and jump up and down. I couldn't hold back the urge, so I did just that! My heart was beating fast, and it seemed to <u>pulsate</u> in time with the driving beat of the music. I could feel the music <u>propel</u> both my friend and me out onto the dance floor. Guess what? She didn't feel so sad anymore!

- I don't understand what <u>compels</u> people to dress up as monsters and ghouls on Halloween. I mean, what makes them want to look as scary as possible? Truth be told, I find some of those costumes downright <u>repulsive</u>. Be that as it may, those gross garbs won't keep me from having fun on this craziest of holidays!

LIST 2

acupuncture
punctilious
punctual
punctuation

punct

punct**ure**

Punct is a Latin root that means "point" or "dot."

- Words containing *punct* usually relate to a point of some kind.
- When you see *punct,* think of **punct**ure (make a hole with a sharp, "pointed" object).

Clues to Meaning Use *punct* as a clue to the meanings of the underlined words.

- Our English teacher expects us to be <u>punctual</u>—on time and in our seats when the bell rings so he can start class right away. He is trying to train us to be <u>punctilious</u> and pay attention to every tiny detail in class. When it comes to writing, he expects our use of <u>punctuation</u> to be perfect. Believe me, we work hard to make sure no periods, commas, or semicolons are in the wrong place!

- Amy heard that <u>acupuncture</u> treatments might make her headaches better. Her doctor could perform the procedure, which involves inserting sharp needles into her skin at particular points.

. . . .

In Your Notebook Write each list word and a brief clue that will help you remember the meaning of the word.

Context Clues

You can use context clues to check the meaning of a word.

1. First, reread the context passage.

2. As you read, replace the word with your understood meaning.

3. Ask yourself, "Does my definition make sense in this passage?"

In the passage about *acupuncture*, the context clues are "inserting sharp needles" and "treatments might make her headaches better." Based on these clues, you can confirm that *acupuncture* is a practice of inserting needles into the body to relieve pain.

Apply and Extend

■ List 1

How does a prefix change the meaning of a word that has the root *pel?* For example, the prefix *ex* means "out."

ex (out) + pel (drive or push) = expel (to drive out)

Write sentences for the words *dispel, propel,* and *expel.* If you wish, use a dictionary to look up the meaning of each prefix.

■ List 1

Write a question about one of the words that contains the root *pel* or *puls,* showing that you understand the meaning of the word. Here is an example question for the word *pulsate: Which word describes the action of expanding and contracting in a steady rhythm?*

■ List 2

The word *punctuation* comes from a medieval Latin word meaning "a marking with points." Write two sentences about two kinds of punctuation marks. Describe what each one looks like and tell when and how to use it.

Word History Choose an interesting word from this week's lesson. What can you find out about the history and origins of your word? Answer the following questions:

- From which language did your word derive?

- What is the first recorded instance of its use in the English language?

- What is one interesting fact you learned about your word?

- List related words that you find.

> **Did you know?**
> The first printed English books used three punctuation marks: the stroke (/), which marked groups of words; the colon (:), which marked a brief pause; and the period (.), which marked the end of a sentence and a brief pause.

bankruptcy
barter
budget
coupon
currency
debit
default
inflation

Use Context as Clues to Meaning

When it comes to money, avoid acting on impulse. Giving in to the urge to buy things you can't afford can lead to *bankruptcy*—a state in which a person no longer has money to pay his or her bills. The word *bankruptcy* has an interesting origin: In the sixteenth century, when moneylenders did business, they sat on a bench. If the moneylender ran out of money, people broke the bench.

bank (bench) + rupt (rupture or break) = bankrupt (broken bench)

The words in this list are related to money. You may come across them in your social studies class.

Read these paragraphs about money. How does the context help you understand the meanings of the underlined words?

- A country can't simply print all of the underline{currency}, or paper money, it wants. Printing too much money makes it worth less and leads to underline{inflation}, or a sharp increase in prices. Before currency became common, many people would underline{barter}, or trade, for what they needed. For example, a farmer might give the blacksmith fresh vegetables, and the blacksmith might shoe the farmer's horses.

- When you write a check or take money from an ATM, your bank will underline{debit} your account, or subtract the amount you took from the total amount you have in the bank.

- When you keep records of what you spend, you can more easily underline{budget} your money in the future, estimating what things will cost based on what they cost in the past. You can save money by using underline{coupons}, which offer discounts or free services or products.

- People who borrow money from a bank have to make regular loan repayments. Anyone who loses a job may underline{default}, or fail to make payments, on a loan. If someone has to file in court for underline{bankruptcy}, the court will tell the companies to which the person owes money that she or he is unable to pay the bills.

In Your Notebook Write the list words. Then choose three words and make a vocabulary concept map for each word.

Using an Online Dictionary

The word *default* has several meanings. To check that you're using the correct meaning of a word, search an online dictionary.

- Enter the word *definition* and the word you are looking for in a search engine.

- Read through each definition and try each one in the sentence you are reading.

- Choose the definition that makes the most sense in the sentence.

In addition to definitions, online dictionaries often provide word origins, example sentences, and audio pronunciations. Bookmark a good online dictionary and use it to look up words.

Have you heard these expressions?
- budget crunch
- balance the budget
- budget shortfall

Apply and Extend

Companies and governments sometimes sell a document called a *bond* to raise money. Use an online reference source to find out what the word *coupon* has to do with these bonds. Write a few sentences explaining the relationship.

The word *budget* comes from a French word meaning "leather bag or pouch." How is this definition related to a modern budget, which involves carefully keeping track of one's money to be sure that one doesn't spend more than one makes? Write two or three sentences answering this question.

Graphic Gallery Use your skills as a cartoonist to create a comic strip using words from this week's lesson. Draw pictures and write dialogue or use an online program to create the graphic text. How many of the words can you use? Work together with classmates to compile the class's comic strips into a Graphic Gallery.

LIST 1 — loq, loc

colloquial
elocution
loquacious
ventriloquist

Loq is a Latin root that means "speak." Another way to spell this root is *loc*.

- Words containing *loq* or *loc* usually have something to do with speaking.
- When you see *loq* or *loc,* think of *eloquent* ("speaks" well).

Clues to Meaning Use *loq* and *loc* as clues to the meanings of the underlined words.

- Martin, the <u>ventriloquist</u>, walked onto the stage with his puppet Jules. Martin had been performing for two years and was good at making it look as if Jules was doing all the talking. Without ever moving his own lips, Martin makes Jules sound <u>loquacious</u>. What a talkative little puppet!

- Sera had been practicing for the speech contest, using everything that her coach had taught her about <u>elocution</u>—to speak clearly and distinctly and to use her voice and hands to make specific points while she talked. She also had to remember not to greet the judges with slang or something <u>colloquial</u> and informal, such as "What's up?" The judges would take off points for that.

LIST 2 — lingu

bilingual
linguine
linguist

Lingu is a Latin root that means "language."

- The word *linguistics* has a Latin root and two suffixes.
  lingu (language) + ist (expert) + ics (study of) = linguistics

When you see *lingu,* think of **lingu**istics (the study of "language" by experts).

Clues to Meaning Use *lingu* as a clue to the meanings of the underlined words.

- The <u>linguist</u> studied several languages in college, and now she can speak four languages fluently. She grew up in a <u>bilingual</u> household, speaking both Italian and English.

- She loves to eat <u>linguine</u>, a kind of pasta. In Italian, the name means "little tongues."

son

dissonance
resonate
sonic
sonorous
unison

Son is a Latin root that means "sound."

- Words containing *son* usually have something to do with sound.
- The word *consonant* has the Latin roots *con* and *son*.
  con (with) + son (sound) + ant = consonant

When you see *son,* think of *consonant* (a speech "sound" that isn't a vowel).

Clues to Meaning Use *son* as a clue to the meanings of the underlined words.

- Greg sang the song in his deep, <u>sonorous</u> voice to get the choir started, but the choir had trouble singing in <u>unison</u>. Why was it so hard for them to sound like they were all one voice? It was rather unpleasant to hear the <u>dissonance</u> of so many voices singing different notes.

- Tim could hear the <u>sonic</u> boom of the plane. His teeth chattered as the thundering sound <u>resonated</u> through his head.

• •

In Your Notebook Write each list word and its meaning.

Using a Thesaurus

To use a printed thesaurus, use the guide words and numbers in the index to find the page that has the word you're looking for. The entry will list parts of speech and various meanings and synonyms. If you're using an online thesaurus such as *thesaurus.com,* you will find antonyms as well as synonyms.

■ List 1

The words *ventriloquist* and *colloquial* have other roots in addition to *loq*. What are they? Look in a dictionary for the words' etymologies. Write a sentence for each word.

■ List 2

Think about how the words *bilingual* and *linguist* are related in meaning. Write a sentence to explain the relationship.

■ List 3

Write a question about one of the words that contains *son,* showing that you understand the meaning of the word. An example is: *Which word describes a quality of an opera singer's voice?*

The Illustrated Word Sharpen your pencils—it's time to play a picture game. Divide a group into two teams. Write lesson words on cards and place them in a stack upside down. The first person on Team 1 takes a card, draws a picture that represents the word on the card, and shows the picture to his or her team. If team members guess the word in 30 seconds, the team gets a point. Now it's Team 2's turn.

Have you heard these terms?
- supersonic
- sonic boom
- bilingual education

LIST WORDS

correlation
extrapolation
rate of change
regression
residual
rise
run
slope

Use Context as Clues to Meaning

Each subject area has its own "language." The list words in this lesson are from the language of math. Some of the words, such as *rise,* are multiple-meaning words. In this lesson, you'll learn what they mean in math.

Read this information about data. How do the graph and context help you understand the meanings of the underlined words?

Is there a relationship, or <u>correlation</u>, between how long you study and the grade you get on a test? Each green point on the graph represents one student. The blue line most closely matches the pattern of the data. Some points fall above the line and some fall below, as shown by the red lines.

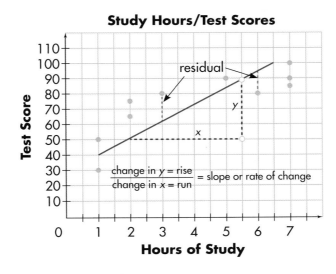

Study Hours/Test Scores

This vertical distance between a green dot and the blue line is called a <u>residual</u>. Drawing the blue line to show a relationship is called a <u>regression</u>.

The relationship between hours of study and test scores is shown by the <u>slope</u> of the line. The vertical purple line shows the change in the *y*-axis, or the <u>rise</u>. The horizontal purple line shows the change in the *x*-axis, or the <u>run</u>. Dividing the rise by the run gives you the <u>slope</u>, or <u>rate of change</u>, of the line. The graph also lets you predict what would happen if you studied for only half an hour. You do this by thinking how the line would look if extended to the left. This is called <u>extrapolation</u>, or estimating a value beyond the measured data.

· ·

In Your Notebook Write the list words. Then draw a graph like the one shown here. Label your graph using as many list words as you can.

Did you know?

The common, or general, meaning of a word can help you understand its meaning in math. When you *rise,* you stand up. You move vertically, similar to the *y*-axis on a graph.

Synonym Study

Knowing the relationship between words can help you better understand the meanings of the words. For example, the mathematics terms *slope* and *rate of change* are synonyms. Both are ratios of the vertical change to the horizontal change and are calculated in the same way: by dividing the rise by the run. Other synonyms in mathematics include *power/exponent, integer/whole number,* and *numerical value/absolute value.*

Apply and Extend

■ The word *extrapolation* begins with the prefix *extra,* which means "outside of" or "beyond." In math, to *extrapolate* means to fill in a gap that is "outside" of the range of measured data. For example, you can extend the line on a graph. As you look at the graph on the previous page, would it make sense to extrapolate the line to the right? Why, or why not? Write one or two sentences answering this question.

■ The words *rise, run,* and *slope* have general meanings in addition to their meanings in math. Use one of the words in a sentence that demonstrates its math-related meaning. Then use the same word in a sentence that demonstrates a general meaning.

Rap It Up Working with a classmate, choose a word from the week's lesson. Use the word and its definition to create a short poem or rap. Compile your rap with other classmates' raps into a Rap It Up notebook.

sol   LIST 1

List 1
- isolate
- sole
- soliloquy
- solitary
- solitude
- soloist

Sol is a Latin root that means "alone."

- Words containing *sol* usually have something to do with being alone.
- When you see *sol,* think of **sol**o (doing something "alone").

Clues to Meaning Use *sol* as a clue to the meanings of the underlined words.

- Living a <u>solitary</u> life and being alone much of the time, as Thoreau was when he lived on Walden Pond, might be satisfying to some people, but it is not healthy to <u>isolate</u> oneself and not see another person for a long period of time.

- Some artists thrive living in <u>solitude</u>, preferring to spend time on their own developing their talents without any outside interference.

- A <u>soloist</u> sings alone or plays an instrument by herself.

- The actor, who was alone on stage, began his <u>soliloquy</u>. In the speech, he expressed his character's thoughts about the events in the play.

- The <u>sole</u> desire of many artists—the only thing those artists want—is to become better at their craft.

cata   LIST 2

List 2
- cataclysm
- catacomb
- catalog
- catalyst
- catastrophe
- catatonic

Cata is a Greek root that means "down."

- Use *cata* as a clue to meaning when you come across words that contain this root.
- When you see *cata,* think of **cata**ract (a steep waterfall tumbling "down").

Clues to Meaning Use *cata* as a clue to the meanings of the underlined words.

- In A.D. 79, Pompeii, Italy, was completely changed by a <u>cataclysm</u>, a terrifying event that involved a volcanic eruption so large that it buried the city and most of its inhabitants in ash.

- Archaeologists did not discover the city or learn about the <u>catastrophe</u> that killed almost everyone until the sixteenth and seventeenth centuries. Now, visitors can see a <u>catalog</u> that lists the artifacts that have been found where the city used to stand.

- When the few people who had managed to escape Pompeii came back, they were shocked and, most likely, <u>catatonic</u>. It is distressing to picture them numb and expressionless as they surveyed the damage.

- Explorers found the remains of many Pompeians who were killed while trying to escape. Incidentally, burying the dead in <u>catacombs</u>, or underground cemeteries, was an ancient Italian custom.

- Natural disasters are often <u>catalysts</u> for social change. If a government responds poorly to a disaster, citizens demand change.

· ·

In Your Notebook Write the list words. Beside each list word write the context clues in the passages that are provided for that word.

Verbal Irony

Irony is a contrast between what is expected and what is actually true. One type of irony is verbal irony, in which a speaker says one thing but means the opposite. An example of verbal irony would be an actor with stage fright saying: "Oh, I can't *wait* to stand in front of an audience and deliver my soliloquy."

■ List 1

Think about how *solitary, soliloquy, isolate,* and *soloist* are related in meaning. Is a solitary person an isolated person? Can a violin soloist perform a soliloquy? Write a few sentences explaining some of the relationships among these words.

■ List 2

Catastrophe and *cataclysm* have similar meanings—they share the Greek root *cata.* The meanings are slightly different, however, because of the other roots in each word. Write a sentence using each word. Use context to show that you understand each word's meaning.

■ List 2

Choose one of the list words and write a sentence that displays verbal irony. Show that you understand the meaning of the word. If you need to check a meaning, use a dictionary.

Clue Review Play a word game with one of your classmates. Choose one of the list words. Give your partner a clue about the word. Did your partner guess the word correctly? If not, provide other clues until your partner correctly identifies the word. Then switch roles.

Did you know?
The word *isolate* comes from the Latin word *insula,* meaning "island." Like an island, you're isolated if you're cut off from others.

LIST WORDS

agonize
audacity
avatar
endure
gallant
resolute
triumph
virtue

Use Context as Clues to Meaning

A hero is a person admired for bravery, nobility, or strength. Some heroes are mythological, and others are real-life, modern people. At times, a hero is the only person who stands between a potential victim and a catastrophe.

The word *catastrophe* has the Greek roots *cata* and *strophe,* which mean "down" and "turn." When you combine the roots, the word means "overturning" and "sudden turn." However, it has come to mean "sudden disaster." Knowing the meaning of *catastrophe* can help you understand the challenges a hero might face. What personal qualities would a man or woman need in order to overcome these challenges? At the left are words that describe a hero.

Read the following descriptions. How does the context help you understand the meanings of the underlined words?

- Sir Lancelot was a brave and <u>gallant</u> knight who was courteous and respectful toward women.

- The Greek hero Odysseus showed <u>audacity</u> when he dared to boldly confront the giant Cyclops, Polyphemus.

- Firefighters do not <u>agonize</u> over whether they should enter a burning building; worrying about their own safety is the last thing on their minds.

- Because they don't give up easily, heroes <u>triumph</u> when others fail.

- Brave and firm heroes are <u>resolute</u>, or determined, in the face of difficult obstacles that might scare other people away.

- The gods assigned Hercules twelve "labors" over twelve years. His incredible strength helped him <u>endure</u> these difficult tasks.

- Modern heroes, such as male and female athletes who are permanently injured but refuse to give up their active lives, are admired for their <u>virtues</u> of confidence, courage, and perseverance.

- Hindus believe that the Hindu god Vishnu took on human form when he came to Earth. In that form, or <u>avatar</u>, he was named Rama. He rescued his wife Sita from a demon.

In Your Notebook Write the list words. Next to each word, write another word or words that you associate with it. As an example, for *audacity* you might write *daring*. If you wish, use a dictionary to check word meanings.

Antonym Study

An antonym is a word that has a meaning that is the opposite of the meaning of another word. For example, *unsure* and *indecisive* are antonyms of the list word *resolute* ("determined"). Antonyms are often used to contrast two things, such as *believable* and *unbelievable* accounts of an event. Antonyms can help increase your vocabulary and make you a stronger reader and writer. To find antonyms for a word, you can look in an online resource such as *thesaurus.com* and choose the antonym that best expresses your intended meaning.

> **Did you know?**
> *Agony,* which is the base word of *agonize,* comes from the Greek word *agōnia,* meaning "public gathering." Ancient Greeks used to have outdoor contests, and the word came to mean any "struggle." Today *agony* means "pain."

Apply and Extend

☐ Think of a hero—real or imaginary. Write a few sentences describing the hero, using several of the list words in a way that shows you understand the meanings of the words.

☐ An antihero is a person or character who does not appear to have the traditional attributes of a hero. What antonyms of the list words can be used to describe antiheroes? If you wish, go online to find examples of antiheroes.

Word History Many of the words you have studied have Latin or Greek roots. The word *avatar* has a different origin. What can you find out about the history and origins of *avatar?* Answer the following questions:

- From which language did the word derive?
- Why is it included in this lesson about words describing heroes?
- What is the word's original meaning?
- What is another way in which the word is used today?
- What is one interesting fact you learned about the word?

LIST 1

corporation
corpulent
corpuscle
incorporate

corp

Corp is a Latin root that means "body."

ANCHOR WORD
corpse

- Words containing *corp* usually have something to do with the human body or with a body of something.

  When you see *corp,* think of **corp**se (a dead "body").

Clues to Meaning Use *corp* as a clue to the meanings of the underlined words.

- Fernando Botero is a famous artist who paints and sculpts animal and human figures with large, bulky, <u>corpulent</u> bodies.

- Red <u>corpuscles</u> are cells in human and animal blood that carry oxygen to the body's tissues.

- The author's interest in sports history led him to <u>incorporate</u> information about the World Series in his book about the 1960s.

- The <u>corporation</u> Rachael worked for was a huge company, with many departments, employees, and branch offices around the world.

LIST 2

psyche
psychiatrist
psychology
psychosomatic

psych

Psych is a Greek root that means "mind" or "spirit."

ANCHOR WORD
psychic

- Words containing *psych* usually have something to do with the mind or spirit of a person.

  When you see *psych,* think of **psych**ic (someone who claims to read your "mind").

Clues to Meaning Use *psych* as a clue to the meanings of the underlined words.

- Dr. Milano trained to be a <u>psychiatrist</u> because she was interested in helping people who have mental or emotional disorders.

- Emily's doctor was unable to find any physical cause for her intense headaches, so he concluded that there was a <u>psychosomatic</u> cause, and that her headaches were probably her body's reaction to stress.

- Georgia took a class in <u>psychology</u> and found it fascinating. She loved learning about human behavior, thoughts, and emotions.

- Nate took time every day to sit quietly and breathe slowly. Doing this calmed his <u>psyche</u>, or his mind and spirit.

physical
physics
physiology
physique

Phys is a Greek root that means "nature" or "natural."

- Words containing *phys* usually have something to do with nature or the natural world.
- When you see *phys,* think of **phys**ician (doctor of "natural" science).

Clues to Meaning Use *phys* as a clue to the meanings of the underlined words.

- Competitive bodybuilders regularly lift weights to build and maintain muscles and a strong <u>physique</u>.

- Liza's sister was studying <u>physiology</u> to learn how all of the parts of the human body work together.

- <u>Physics</u> is a branch of science that studies relationships between matter and energy and includes the study of light, sound, heat, mechanics, electricity, magnetism, and atomic energy.

- At Pete's <u>physical</u>, the doctor weighed him, measured him, checked his blood pressure, and asked about his overall health.

• •

In Your Notebook Use each list word in a sentence that contains at least one context clue to the word's meaning.

Figurative Language

Figurative language uses words in a non-literal way to compare two unlike things. For example, a corporation is a business; it is not human. But in the following sentence a corporation is being personified: "The corporation shrugged off its losses." Shrugging off losses is something a person might do. People can shrug, but corporations can't! Personification is one type of figurative language.

Apply and Extend

Did you know?

In Greek and Roman mythology, Psyche was a human girl who became the wife of Eros, the god of love. She later became a goddess who personified the soul.

■ List 1

Work with a partner and choose two list words. One partner writes a sentence that shows one meaning of one word, while the other partner writes a sentence that shows one meaning of the other word. Then challenge each other to say a sentence that shows that you know what your partner's word means.

■ List 2

Write a sentence, using context to point to the meaning of one of the list words. Then black out the word and ask a classmate if he or she can identify the word from the context you have created. Take turns reading each other's sentences.

■ List 3

Think about how *physical, physiology,* and *physique* are related in meaning. Is a physique physical? If you study physiology, do you study about a physique? Write a sentence or two, using these three words.

Rap It Up Working with a classmate, choose a word from the week's lesson. Use the word and its definition to create a short poem or rap. Compile your rap with other classmates' raps into a Rap It Up notebook.

Incorporate

E pluribus unum—
You know what I'm saying?
Out of many, one—
It's the motto of our nation.
We have to work together
'Cause we share one common fate.
So come on, people, In-cor-por-ate!

LIST WORDS

accent
biographical
ellipsis
exaggeration
excerpt
inflection
pronunciation
stress

Use Context as Clues to Meaning

When you write, you have to make choices, many choices. For example, imagine you are writing a biographical work, or a story of someone's life. What details of that person's life should you incorporate? How will you describe your subject's physical appearance and psychological traits? Answering these questions will help you craft an engaging biographical work.

The word *biographical* has the Greek roots *bio* and *graph* and the suffix *ical*.

bio (life) + graph (write) + ical (of) = biographical (of or about someone's life)

Whether you are writing a biography or another type of text, you use certain words to talk about your subject. At the right are words related to writing. You may come across them in your language arts class.

Read the passage about writing. How does the context help you understand the meanings of the underlined words?

In a <u>biographical</u> work, an author can tell the story of someone's life by incorporating letters written to or by the subject and interviews with people who knew the subject. The author might <u>excerpt</u> short quotes from longer passages, using <u>ellipses</u> (a series of dots, like this: . . .) to show where text has been omitted. Some authors overstate descriptions of events to make their writing more interesting or dramatic. An example of <u>exaggeration</u> is describing an ordinary snowfall as a raging blizzard.

An author often includes the names of key places in the subject's life and the names of people who significantly influenced the subject. If any of these names are uncommon, she looks them up in a dictionary and notes their <u>pronunciation</u> so readers know how to say the names. Doing this helps her fully integrate the names of people and places that are important in the book she is writing. As she writes, she notes what syllable the <u>accent</u> lands on and says that accented syllable with greater force, or <u>stress</u>. She also notes the <u>inflection</u>, or the changes in the pitch of her own voice as she reads her work aloud. She knows that changing her <u>inflection</u> can change the meaning of a sentence.

· ·

In Your Notebook Write each list word and a sentence for it that shows you understand the word's meaning.

Did you know?

The word *accent* derives from a Latin word meaning "song added." Accents, like songs, change the way words sound by adding force or by making sounds higher or lower.

Multiple Meanings

As you read you may come across words that have different meanings from the ones you're used to. For example, you might know the word *accent* as a noun that describes the way in which people in a different part of the country pronounce words. But *accent* can also be a verb: "That red fabric *accents* the color on the walls." The word *stress* also has multiple meanings. *Stress* can be a noun: "I am under a lot of *stress*!" And *stress* can be a verb: "I want to *stress* the fact that tomorrow we have the End-of-the-Year Spelling Test!"

Apply and Extend

■ The word *excerpt* can be used as a noun and as a verb. Write one sentence using the word as a noun and another sentence using it as a verb.

■ The words *exaggeration* and *pronunciation* are nouns, but they can be changed into verbs: *exaggerate* and *pronounce*. Write one sentence using *exaggerate* and another sentence using *pronounce*. Consult a dictionary to check the different meanings of these nouns and verbs.

Clue Review Play a word game with one of your classmates. Choose one of the list words. Give your partner a clue about the word. Did your partner guess the word correctly? If not, provide another clue until your partner correctly identifies the word. Then switch roles.

ject

LIST 1

conjecture
dejected
inject
objection

Ject is a Latin root that means "throw."

- Words containing *ject* usually have something to do with throwing.
- When you see *ject,* think of *eject* ("throw" out).

Clues to Meaning Use *ject* as a clue to the meanings of the underlined words.

"Your Honor," said the public defender, "the prosecution is making a <u>conjecture</u> without presenting any evidence."

"I agree," said the judge, turning to the prosecutor. "We do not guess here, counsel. Do you have any <u>objection</u> to continuing?"

"No," the prosecutor replied. "I will go on and present evidence."

The defendant frowned and slumped in her chair, feeling <u>dejected</u> about the trial. She wished that she could <u>inject</u> a comment of her own, but she knew that she was not allowed to interrupt.

• •

ab

LIST 2

abdicate
abduction
abhorrent
abolish

Ab is a Latin prefix that means "off," "away," or "down."

- Use *ab* as a clue to meaning when you come across words that contain this prefix.
- When you see *ab,* think of *absent* (being "away").

Clues to Meaning Use *ab* as a clue to the meanings of the underlined words.

- In 1936, King Edward VIII of Great Britain decided to <u>abdicate</u>, giving up the throne so he could marry an American woman.

- Some people have claimed to be victims of an alien <u>abduction</u>, saying aliens kidnapped them and took them away to a spaceship.

- The vegetarian shuddered with disgust at the <u>abhorrent</u> thought of eating meat.

- Supporters of the movement to <u>abolish</u> slavery in the United States argued that slavery was immoral and should be done away with.

• •

LIST 3 — chrom

chromium
chromosome
chromosphere
monochromatic

ANCHOR WORD
chrome

Chrom is a Greek root that means "color."

- Words containing *chrom* usually have something to do with color.
- When you see *chrom,* think of *chrome* (a silvery "color" on cars).

Clues to Meaning Use *chrom* as a clue to the meanings of the underlined words.

- Chromium, a grayish metallic element, is used for making dyes and paints, such as chrome red and chrome yellow.

- Chromosomes are rod-shaped bodies in the nucleus of a cell that contain genetic information. Chromosomes can be dyed a color and studied under a microscope.

- The chromosphere is the red-hot layer of gas around the sun.

- Some houses are painted with several colors, but others have only one color, giving them a monochromatic appearance.

• •

In Your Notebook Write each list word and its meaning. You may want to consult a dictionary to confirm meanings.

Context Clues

Use context clues to verify the meaning of an unfamiliar word. A context clue is text near the unfamiliar word that gives clues about its meaning. In the sentence that follows, the words *certain* and *guess* are context clues to the meaning of the underlined word *conjecture.*

The president wanted to be absolutely certain that she was making the right decision; however, all she could do was guess and make a conjecture about the outcome.

Apply and Extend

■ List 1

Choose a list word. Explain how the root *ject* relates to its meaning. Then write a sentence using the word, creating context that shows you understand its meaning.

■ List 2

Choose two list words. Think of a synonym (a word with a similar meaning) for each word and write a sentence using the synonym. Challenge a partner to identify the list words that could replace the synonyms.

Have you heard these expressions?
- Your honor, I have an objection!
- Objection sustained!

■ List 3

Many words with the root *chrom* are used in the field of photography. Use *monochromatic* in a sentence about photography. Try to use other words that have the root *chrom*.

Skit Work with a small group to brainstorm the idea of an alien *abduction*. Some students can claim to be victims. Others can play the roles of a police officer, a doctor, a reporter, and so on—maybe even an alien! Encourage students to use the words *abduct* and *abductor* as well as *abduction*.

LESSON 56 **Domain-Specific Vocabulary**
Science

LIST WORDS

chlorophyll
oxygen
photosynthesis
pistil
pollination
stamen
starch
tropism

Use Context as Clues to Meaning

In your science class, you learn about plants and animals. From cell structure in animals to photosynthesis in plants, you learn about living things.

The word *photosynthesis* has the Greek roots *photo* and *syn*.

photo (light) + syn (together) = photosynthesis (process in which light, together with other elements, creates food for plants)

Photosynthesis is certainly an important word in the study of plants. At the left are more words related to plants, which you may come across in your science class.

Read this information about plants. How does the context help you understand the meanings of the underlined words?

Did you know that without plants we would be unable to survive? Plants release <u>oxygen</u> into the air. <u>Oxygen</u> is a gas that is part of Earth's atmosphere and that people and animals breathe to survive.

Each plant has a <u>stamen</u>, which is the male part of the flower. It produces pollen, a sticky powder. Each plant also has a <u>pistil</u>, the female part of the flower. During <u>pollination</u>, pollen is transferred from the stamen to the pistil. The pollen can be carried by the wind or animals, such as bees and birds. These animals get pollen on their wings and beaks, which rubs off on the top of the pistils. This process of <u>pollination</u> produces the plant's seeds.

In a process called <u>tropism</u>, plants move toward light, gravity, or moisture as they grow. <u>Tropism</u> is what causes a plant's leaves to face the sun. In another process called <u>photosynthesis</u>, plants make food in their leaves using water and carbon dioxide in the presence of light and <u>chlorophyll</u>, a green pigment that helps leaves absorb energy from light. During <u>photosynthesis</u>, a chemical called <u>starch</u> is created—and this is one way that plants store food.

In Your Notebook Write the list words. Next to each word, briefly explain its part in the world of plants.

Word Roots and Affixes

Many words used in science have Greek roots. Two Greek roots, *chloros* and *phyllos,* make up the word *chlorophyll.* If you look in a dictionary, you will find that *chloros* means "green" and *phyllon* means "leaf." Knowing this, you can make a conjecture that the meaning of the word *chlorophyll* is "green in leaves."

Many affixes—prefixes at the beginning of words and suffixes at the end of words—provide clues to the meaning of a word. For example, the suffix *ation* means "an act" or "a process." When added to the word *pollen*, it becomes *pollination*—the process of spreading pollen.

You can find several lists of roots and affixes online. Consulting these lists can help you determine the meaning of many unfamiliar words.

Did you know?
- If you hang a plant upside down, it will grow upright!
- A pitcher plant can eat a lizard!
- Some floating leaves can support the weight of a person!

Apply and Extend

- Research the process of photosynthesis. Then write a few sentences about it, using at least two of the list words and other vocabulary you have learned.

- *Tropism* comes from the Greek *tropos,* which means "to turn." Explain how the meaning of the root relates to the definition of *tropism* and give an example of it. *Tropism* is the moving or growth of an organism (usually a plant) toward light, heat, and water.

Word Match With a partner, write the eight list words on separate cards and then write their basic definitions on separate cards. Mix up the cards and place them face down on a desk. Take turns matching a list word (*chlorophyll, oxygen, photosynthesis, pistil, pollination, stamen, starch, tropism*) with its definition (for example, *stamen* and "male part of the flower").

LIST 1

archetype
prototype
stereotype
typecast
typical
typist
typographical
typography

typ

Typ is a Greek root that means "strike" or "make an impression."

- Words containing *typ* usually have something to do with striking or making an impression.

When you see *typ,* think of *typewriter* (a machine with keys that "strike" and "make an impression" of letters on paper).

Clues to Meaning Use *typ* as a clue to the meanings of the underlined words.

- The <u>typist</u> was striking the keys on his laptop so fast that he made several <u>typographical</u> errors. However, he did fix the mistakes he had typed before turning in the report.

- Mike put the finishing touches on the <u>prototype</u> for the company's newest product. The model had the company's name on it, but Mike thought the <u>typography</u> would be better if the lettering was larger and bolder.

- The actress was tired of playing the part of a jealous sister. "I'm exactly what the audience expects me to be. I'm the <u>stereotype</u> of a jealous sister," she told her agent. "You know, I'd rather play another character. Why do I keep getting <u>typecast</u> in the same role over and over again?"

- *Survivor,* a TV show about people trying to win a contest in a distant part of the world, was never a <u>typical</u> TV show. In fact, it was so different that it became the <u>archetype</u> for other reality shows that awarded big prizes. Other reality show competitions are, in many ways, copies of *Survivor.*

tort

distort
extort
retort
tortuous

Tort is a Latin root that means "twist."

- Words containing *tort* usually have something to do with twisting something.

When you see *tort,* think of *con**tort**ionist* (a performer who can "twist" his or her body into different positions).

Clues to Meaning Use *tort* as a clue to the meanings of the underlined words.

"How was the movie?" Meg's father asked.

"We had to wait 20 minutes to buy our tickets, standing in a <u>tortuous</u> line that wound around the building!" Meg replied rather dramatically.

"A popular movie!" exclaimed her father.

"Actually," Meg said, "the line was long because a man outside the theater was trying to <u>extort</u> money from customers by selling phony movie tickets."

"How unfair of him to try to trick the customers like that," he said.

Meg continued, "When the cashier told him to leave, he angrily <u>retorted</u> that she was lying. Obviously, he was trying to <u>distort</u> the truth by twisting the facts. A manager finally arrived and took control of the situation. But we missed the previews!"

• •

In Your Notebook Write each list word and a sentence using it.

Mythological Allusions

An allusion is a brief, often indirect reference to a person, a place, or an event in literature. Some allusions refer to Greek and Roman myths. For example, an allusion to the "labors of Hercules" suggests a task that requires superhuman qualities. The list word *archetype* can be used to describe Hercules, who is an archetype of a hero, an ideal model upon whom other heroes are copied or based.

149

Apply and Extend

Did you know?

What a difference a letter makes! Be careful not to confuse *tortuous* ("winding") with *torturous* ("extremely painful").

■ List 1

Work with a partner to solve "What Am I?" riddles: "I type keys on a keyboard. What am I?" "I am a model for others that will come after me. What am I?" Solve these riddles and then create other list-word riddles you can exchange with your partner.

■ List 1

Choose three of your favorite *typ* list words and include them in a humorous or serious sentence.

■ List 2

Write one sentence using as many of the list words as you can. Challenge yourself. Can you use all four words in one sentence?

Word Part Invention How much of a wordsmith are you? With a partner, combine word parts from this lesson with other letters or syllables to invent a new word. Then write a definition for your word based on the meanings of the word parts. Share the word and its definition with classmates.

development
elevation
excavate
hinterland
metropolis
sprawl
tract
zoning

Use Context as Clues to Meaning

The word *prototype* has two parts: *proto,* which means "first," and *type*, which means "impression." A prototype is a model, or an original. Did you know that cities have prototypes? For instance, architects and developers create prototypes, such as model homes, to show people what buildings and urban areas might look like after they have been built. At the right are words related to cities. You may come across these words in your social studies class.

The word *metropolis,* which is a large city, has the Greek roots *meter* and *polis*.

meter (mother) + polis (city) = metropolis (mother city; a very large and densely populated city)

Read about the growth of New York City. How does the context help you understand the meanings of the underlined words?

New York City wasn't always the huge, sprawling, densely populated <u>metropolis</u> it is today. The city began as a Dutch trading center, called New Amsterdam, at the southern tip of the island of Manhattan. (Can you find it on a map?) This part of Manhattan is at a lower <u>elevation</u>, or height, than the rest of the island and is, therefore, very vulnerable or susceptible to flooding. As urban <u>development</u> progressed and New York City expanded northward, engineers began to <u>excavate</u>, or carve out, underground tunnels so they could construct a vast subway system beneath the city. In the center of Manhattan a huge <u>tract</u>, or area, of land was set aside for Central Park, which for more than 100 years has given New Yorkers and tourists from around the world relief from the hustle and bustle and noise of the city. Throughout Manhattan, <u>zoning</u> laws have restricted the numbers and types of buildings, and their uses.

Because Manhattan is an island, there is a limited amount of land on which it can grow. Urban <u>sprawl</u> has led to the expansion of population centers away from Manhattan, such as those found in the New York City boroughs of Queens, Brooklyn, Staten Island, and the Bronx. Fewer and fewer of these <u>hinterlands</u>, or remote areas in the region, exist; and, as a result, undeveloped areas are becoming more difficult to find.

• •

In Your Notebook Write each list word and its meaning. Note that some of these words have more than one meaning.

Did you know?

You can impress your dentist on your next visit! The words *excavate* and *cavity* share the Latin root *cavus,* which means "hollow."

Connotation and Denotation

A word's denotation is its literal, exact definition. For example, the denotation of *expand* is "to increase in size," and the denotation of *sprawl* is "to spread out in an irregular manner."

A word's connotation is what is suggested or implied beyond a word's literal meaning. Connotations can be either positive or negative. For example, the word *expand* has a positive connotation, whereas the word *sprawl* has a negative connotation because it suggests uncontrolled growth.

Apply and Extend

■ What is your town or city like? What is its history? Write a few sentences about where you live, using as many of the list words as possible.

■ Choose three words from the word list. For each word, write a sentence that includes context clues for the word. Leave a blank for the word, and ask a classmate to choose the correct word from the word list.

Clue Review Play a word game with one of your classmates. Choose one of the list words. Give your partner a clue about the word. Did your partner guess the word correctly? If not, provide another clue until your partner correctly identifies the word. Then switch roles.

centr — LIST 1

centrifuge
concentrate
concentric
decentralize
eccentric
ethnocentric

Centr is a Latin root that means "center."

- Words containing *centr* usually have something to do with the center or middle of something.

When you see *centr,* think of **cent**er ("center").

Clues to Meaning Use *centr* as a clue to the meanings of the underlined words.

- Have you ever dropped a pebble into the water and watched the <u>concentric</u> circles of ripples that spread out from the center point, where the pebble went in?

- I think we should <u>concentrate</u> our efforts and focus our attention on finding the treasure. Later, we can decide how to divide the goods.

- People who are <u>ethnocentric</u> think they are superior to people from other countries and cultures.

- The painter had a reputation for being <u>eccentric</u>. He behaved in unusual ways and had a sense of humor that some might call "off-center."

- A salad spinner is a kind of <u>centrifuge</u>—as it spins, the water is removed from the lettuce so that the lettuce is crisp.

- The students liked the new <u>decentralized</u> organization of the classroom. The learning centers were no longer in the center of the room.

meter — LIST 2

altimeter
barometer
diameter
metronome
parameter
speedometer

Meter is a Greek root that means "measure."

- Words containing *meter* usually have something to do with measurement.
- The word *millimeter* has the Latin root *milli* and the Greek root *meter*.

milli (thousand) + meter (measure) = millimeter

When you see *meter,* think of *milli**meter*** (unit of length that "measures" 1/1000th of a meter).

Clues to Meaning Use *meter* as a clue to the meanings of the underlined words.

- A pilot frequently checks the <u>altimeter</u>, an instrument in the plane that measures the altitude of the aircraft.

- The weather forecaster uses an instrument called a <u>barometer</u> to measure air pressure.

- Alicia measured the buttons. The <u>diameter</u>, or the measure of each button's width, had to be small enough to fit through the buttonholes.

- Roberto practiced so much for his piano recital that he heard the <u>metronome</u> in his dreams, ticking away, measuring time and keeping the beat for him as he played.

- The <u>parameters</u> of space and time are factors for astronomers and physicists to consider when making calculations.

- The dial on the <u>speedometer</u> in Uncle Jon's car started measuring speed incorrectly, so he immediately drove his car to a mechanic to have it fixed.

In Your Notebook Write a sentence for each list word. Include at least one context clue to the word's meaning.

Synonym Study

A synonym is a word with the same or nearly the same meaning as another word. However, there are different nuances, or shades of meaning, between synonyms. For example, *odd* and *weird* are both synonyms for *eccentric,* but *odd* means "peculiar" and *weird* means "wild." You should consider a word's connotation, or what is suggested beyond its literal meaning, when deciding which synonym to use. Understanding precise meanings will make you a better reader and writer.

Apply and Extend

■ List 1

Choose two or three list words and write sentences that explain how the words have something to do with the center or middle of something.

■ List 1

Write a sentence about one of the words, showing that you understand its meaning (and its root). An example is: *When an organization decentralizes, it no longer has one department that is at the center of everything, and in charge of all the other departments.*

■ List 2

Imagine that you are a weather reporter. Write one or two sentences describing how you would use a barometer to measure the weather.

Graphic Gallery Use your skills as a cartoonist to create a comic strip using words from this week's lesson. Draw pictures and write dialogue or use an online program to create the graphic text. How many of the words can you use? Work together with classmates to compile the class's comic strips into a Graphic Gallery.

Did you know?
Astronauts prepare for the g-forces of a space launch by training on a centrifuge. The centrifuge spins around in a horizontal circle, and the astronauts-in-training feel like they weigh 6.2 times their normal weight! Want to try it?

LIST WORDS

binomial
outlier
parabola
polynomial
quadratic
 function
square root
standard
 deviation
vertex

Use Context as Clues to Meaning

How does a centrifuge work? How do meteorologists measure changes in barometric pressure? Math can help you answer these questions. At the left are words related to math. You may come across these words in your math class.

The word *binomial* has the prefix *bi*, the Latin root *nomen,* and the suffix *ial*.

bi (two) + nomen (name) + ial (a form of) = binomial (an algebraic expression with two terms)

Read the following about the list words in this lesson. How do the context clues, expressions, and equations help you understand the meanings of the underlined words?

- A binomial is a math expression with two terms, which can be constants, variables, and exponents.

    Example: $5x^3 - 3$

- A polynomial is a math expression with two or more terms. A binomial is a type of polynomial.

    Example: $5x^3 - 3 + \frac{1}{2}$

- The standard form of a quadratic function is $y = ax^2 + bx + c$, where $a \neq 0$.

- The graph of a quadratic function is a parabola, a *U*-shaped curve. The vertex of a parabola is its highest point that opens down. If the parabola opens up, the vertex is the lowest point.

- A square root is a number that, when multiplied by itself, produces a given number. For example, $4 \times 4 = 16$, so the square root of 16 is 4.

- An outlier is a value that is a good deal lesser or greater than most of the other values in a set of data. For example, in the scores 5, 30, 32, 33, 35, 37, 39, 57, both 5 and 57 are outliers.

- A standard deviation is a measure of how spread out a set of numbers are.

· ·

In Your Notebook Write the list words. Next to each word, give an example or draw a diagram to show you understand its meaning.

Etymology Study

Did you know that the word *parabola* has the same origin as the word *parable*? What could a *U*-shaped curve and a story that teaches a moral lesson have in common? Both words come from the Greek word *parabolē*, which means "placing side by side," or "comparison." In many cases, a parable compares one character's behavior to that of another. A parabola is symmetric. You can draw a line down the center of a parabola and create two equal parts.

The words *parable* and *parabola* are "doublets." That is, they are two words with different meanings derived from the same roots.

Apply and Extend

■ The prefix *bi* means "two"; the prefix *poly* means "many." How do these prefixes help you understand the meanings of the words *binomial* and *polynomial?* Write a sentence that explains the relationship between a binomial and a polynomial.

■ Write one or two sentences that explain the relationships among a quadratic function, a parabola, and a vertex.

Clue Review Play a word game with one of your classmates. Choose one of the list words. Give your partner a clue about the word. Did your partner guess the word correctly? If not, provide another clue until your partner correctly identifies the word. Then switch roles.

Did you know?
Algebra was invented by Muhammad ibn al-Khowarizmi (born about 780), an Iraqi mathematician. *Algebra* comes from the Arabic word *al-jabr*, which means "reunion of broken parts."

How to Use This Glossary

This glossary can help you understand and pronounce the words in this book. The entries in this glossary are in alphabetical order. There are guide words at the top of each page to show you the first and last words on the page. A pronunciation key is at the bottom of the following page.

1   2   3

glos·sar·y (glos′ ər ē), *n.*, list of special, technical, or hard words, usually in alphabetical order, with explanations or comments: *a glossary of terms used in chemistry. Textbooks sometimes have glossaries at the end. n., pl.* **glos·sar·ies.** — 5

6 [**Glossary** comes from a Greek word meaning "tongue." The Greeks used *tongue* to mean "a language." Eventually this Greek word came to mean "an explanation" of hard words.]

1 *The entry word is in dark type. It shows how the word is spelled and how the word is divided into syllables.*

2 *The pronunciation is in parentheses. It also shows which syllables are stressed.*

3 *The part-of-speech label shows the function of an entry word and any listed form of that word.*

4 *The definition and examples show you what the word means and how it is used.*

5 *Inflected, irregular, and other special forms are shown to help you use the word correctly.*

6 *The etymology is in brackets and gives the origin of the entry word.*

Aa

ab·bre·vi·a·tion (ə brē′vē ā′shən), *n.* **1.** a shortened form of a word or phrase standing for a whole: *"Dr." is an abbreviation for "Doctor."* **2.** act of making briefer.

ab·di·cate (ab′də kāt), *v.* to give up or formally renounce office, power, or authority; resign: *When the king abdicated his throne, his brother became king. v.* **ab·di·cat·ed, ab·di·cat·ing. –ab′di·ca′tion,** *n.* **–ab′di·ca′tor,** *n.*

ab·duc·tion (ab dukt′shen), *n.* the carrying off of a person by force or by trickery; a kidnapping. **–ab·duc′tor,** *n.*

ab·hor·rent (ab hôr′ənt), *adj.* causing horror; disgusting; hateful: *Lying and stealing are abhorrent to someone who is honest.* **–ab·hor′rent·ly,** *adv.*

ab·lu·tion (ab lü′shən), *n.* act of washing or cleansing the body, especially as part of a religious ceremony.

a·bode (ə bōd′), **1.** *n.* place to live in; dwelling; house: *A simple hut was their abode.* **2.** *v.* a past tense and a past participle of **abide:** *She abode there one year.*

a·bol·ish (ə bol′ish), *v.* to do away with completely; put an end to: *Many people wish that nations would abolish war.* **–a·bol′ish·a·ble,** *adj.* **–a·bol′ish·er,** *n.* **–a·bol′ish·ment,** *n.*

a·byss (ə bis′), *n.* **1.** a bottomless or very great depth; a very deep crack in the Earth: *The mountain climber stood at the edge of a cliff overlooking an abyss four thousand feet deep.* **2.** anything too deep or great to be measured; lowest depth: *an abyss of despair. n., pl.* **a·byss·es.** [**Abyss** comes from a Latin word meaning "without bottom."]

ac·cent (ak′sent), *n.* **1.** greater voice or stronger tone of voice used in pronouncing some syllables or words: *In "letter," the accent is on the first syllable.* **2.** a mark (′) written or printed to show the spoken force of a syllable, as in *to·day* (tə dā′); stress mark; accent mark. Some words have two accents, a primary or stronger accent (′) and a secondary or weaker accent (′), as in *ac·cel·e·ra·tor* (ak sel′ə rā′tər). [**Accent** comes from a Latin word meaning "song added." An accent changes the way a word is said by adding force or by changing the highness or lowness of sounds, as in songs.]

ac·cred·it·ed (ə kred′ə tid), *adj.* recognized as coming up to an official standard: *Some colleges will accept without examination the graduates of accredited high schools.*

ac·ro·nym (ak′rə nim), *n.* word formed from the first letters or syllables of other words. EXAMPLE: *scuba (self-contained underwater breathing apparatus).*

act (akt), **1.** *v.* to perform on the stage, in movies, on TV, or over the radio; play a part: *He acts the part of the district attorney. She acts very well.* **2.** *n.* a main division of a play or opera: *Most modern plays have three acts.* **–act′a·ble,** *adj.*

ac·u·punc·ture (ak′yů pungk′chər), *n.* an ancient Chinese practice of inserting needles into certain parts of the body. Acupuncture is used to treat some diseases and to relieve pain.

a·cute (ə kyüt′), *adj.* **1.** describes an angle less than a right angle. **2.** sharp and severe.

ad·age (ad′ij), *n.* a wise saying that has been much used; proverb. "Haste makes waste" is a well-known adage.

ad·junct (aj′ungkt), *n.* something added that is less important or not necessary, but helpful: *A greenhouse formed an adjunct to the back porch.*

ad·um·brate (ad əm′brāt), *v.* **1.** to darken or partially cover up. **2.** overshadow.

aer·ate (âr′āt), *v.* **1.** to expose to and mix with air: *Water in this reservoir is aerated and purified by being sprayed high into the air.* **2.** to expose to chemical action with oxygen: *Blood is aerated in the lungs. v.* **aer·at·ed, aer·at·ing.** **–aer·a′tion,** *n.* **–aer′a·tor,** *n.*

aer·i·al (âr′ē əl), *adj.* **1.** of or with aircraft: *aerial photography.* **2.** of or about the air; atmospheric: *aerial currents.* **–aer′i·al·ly,** *adv.*

aer·o·dy·nam·ic (âr′ō dī nam′ik), *adj.* capable of moving easily through air or other gases.

aer·o·nau·tics (âr′ə nȯ′tiks), *n.* science of the design, manufacture, and operation of aircraft.

aer·o·sol (âr′ə sol), *n.* **1.** very fine particles of a solid or liquid substance suspended in the air or in some other gas. Smoke and fog are aerosols. **2.** product packaged under pressure to be released as a spray or mist.

aer·o·space (âr′ō spās), **1.** *n.* Earth's atmosphere and nearby outer space. **2.** *adj.* of aircraft or spacecraft: *the aerospace industry.*

af·flu·ence (af′lü əns), *n.* wealth; riches: *The United States is a country of great affluence.*

ag·nos·tic (ag nos′tik), *adj.* programmed to be compatible with any computer operating system **–ag·nost′i·cal·ly,** *adv.*

ag·o·nize (ag′ə nīz), *v.* to feel great pain; suffer agony: *The lost skiers agonized in the freezing cold for hours. v.* **ag·o·nized, ag·o·niz·ing.**

a·grar·ian (ə grâr′ē ən), *adj.* **1.** of or about farming land, its use, or its ownership: *Most old countries had agrarian disputes between tenants and landlords.* **2.** for the support and advancement of farmers or farming: *an agrarian movement.*

ag·ri·busi·ness (ag′rə biz′nis), *n.* the business of producing, processing, and distributing farm products, especially as carried on by large corporations. *n., pl.* **ag·ri·busi·ness·es.**

a·gron·o·my (ə gron′ə mē), *n.* science of managing farmland; branch of agriculture that deals with crop production. **–a·gron′o·mist,** *n.*

al·tim·e·ter (al tim′ə tər), *n.* device for measuring altitude. Altimeters are used in aircraft.

am·biv·a·lent (am biv′ə lənt), *adj.* acting in opposite ways; having or showing conflicting feelings: *He has an ambivalent attitude toward his friend; he likes him but always quarrels with him.* **–am·biv′a·lent·ly,** *adv.*

a·nach·ro·nism (ə nak′rə niz′əm), *n.* **1.** act of placing anything in some time where it does not belong. It would be an anachronism to show Abraham Lincoln in an automobile. **2.** something placed or occurring out of its proper time. A famous anachronism in Shakespeare's *Julius Caesar* is a striking clock. The Romans had no such clocks. [**Anachronism** comes from the Greek words meaning "back" and "time." Anachronisms usually involve showing something too early in time, in a period before it existed.]

an·gle (ang′gəl), *n.* **1.** the space between two lines or surfaces that meet. **2.** the figure formed by two such lines or surfaces.

an·te·di·lu·vi·an (an′ti də lü′vē ən), *adj.* **1.** very old; old-fashioned. **2.** before the Flood.

an·ti·dote (an′ti dōt), *n.* **1.** medicine or remedy that counteracts the harmful effects of a poison: *Milk is an antidote for some poisons.* **2.** remedy for anything that is harmful: *Education is an antidote for ignorance.*

an·ti·gen (an′tə jən), *n.* any foreign substance, such as a protein or carbohydrate, that causes the body to produce antibodies to counteract it.

a in *hat*	o in *hot*	ch in *child*
ā in *age*	ō in *open*	ng in *long*
â in *care*	ȯ in *all*	sh in *she*
ä in *far*	ô in *order*	th in *thin*
e in *let*	oi in *oil*	ᴛʜ in *then*
ē in *equal*	ou in *out*	zh in *measure*
ėr in *term*	u in *cup*	ə = a in *about*
i in *it*	ů in *put*	ə = e in *taken*
ī in *ice*	ü in *rule*	ə = i in *pencil*

GLOSSARY

an·tip·a·thy (an tip′ə thē), *n.* **1.** a strong dislike; a feeling against: *He felt an antipathy to snakes.* **2.** anything that arouses such a feeling. *n., pl.* **an·tip·a·thies** for 2.

an·tiph·o·nal (an tif′ə nəl), *adj.* related to singing or chanting in which one person or group prays or sings and another person or group answers. –**an·tiph′o·nal·ly**, *adv.*

ap·a·thy (ap′ə thē), *n.* **1.** lack of interest or desire for action; indifference: *The citizens' apathy to local affairs resulted in poor government.* **2.** lack of feeling: *She reacted to her former friend's troubles with apathy.* [**Apathy** comes from Greek words meaning "without feeling."]

a·pex (ā′peks), *n.* **1.** the highest point; tip; *The apex of a triangle is the point opposite the base.* **2.** climax: *Her role in that film was the apex of her career. n., pl.* **a·pex·es** or **ap·i·ces.**

ap·pend·age (ə pen′dij), *n.* thing attached to something larger or more important; addition. Arms, tails, fins, legs, etc., are appendages.

ap·per·tain (ap′ər tān′), *v.* to belong as a part; be connected; relate: *Forestry appertains to geography, to botany, and to agriculture.*

ap·prox·i·mate (ə prok′sə mit *for adj.;* ə prok′sə māt *for verb*), **1.** *adj.* nearly correct: *The approximate length of a meter is 40 inches; the exact length is 39.37 inches.* **2.** *v.* to come near to; approach: *Your account of what happened approximates the truth, but there are several small errors. v.* **ap·prox·i·mat·ed, ap·prox·i·mat·ing.** –**ap·prox′i·mate·ly**, *adv.*

aq·ua·naut (ak′wə nôt), *n.* an underwater explorer.

a·quat·ic (ə kwat′ik *or* ə kwät′ik), *adj.* **1.** growing or living in water: *Water lilies are aquatic plants.* **2.** taking place in or on water: *Swimming and sailing are aquatic sports.*

aq·ue·duct (ak′wə dukt), *n.* **1.** an artificial channel or large pipe for bringing water from a distance. **2.** structure that supports such a channel or pipe.

aq·ui·fer (ak′wə fər), *n.* a wide layer of underground earth or rock that contains water.

arc (ärk), *n.* **1.** any part or the circumference of a circle. **2.** any part of any curved line. [**Arc** comes from a Latin word meaning "an arch" or "a bow." The words **arch** and **archery** also come from this Latin word.]

ar·che·type (är′kə tīp), *n.* an original model or pattern from which copies are made, or out of which later forms develop; prototype: *Last year's fall festival will serve as the archetype for this year's.*

as·sent (ə sent′), **1.** *v.* to agree; consent: *Everyone assented to the plan.* **2.** *n.* acceptance of a proposal, statement, etc.; agreement: *She gave her assent to the plan.*

au·dac·i·ty (ô das′ə tē), *n.* **1.** boldness; reckless daring: *The highest trapeze could not daunt the acrobat's audacity.* **2.** rude boldness; impudence: *They had the audacity to go to the party without being invited.*

aux·il·iar·y (ôg zil′yər ē), *adj.* **1.** giving help or support; assisting: *Some sailboats have auxiliary engines.* **2.** additional: *The main library has several auxiliary branches. n., pl.* **aux·il·iar·ies.**

a·va·tar (av′ə tär′), *n.* (in Hindu mythology) an appearance of a god or goddess on Earth in bodily form; incarnation.

Bb

bac·te·ri·a (bak tir′ē ə), *n., pl.* very tiny and simple living things, so small they can usually be seen only through a microscope. They are single cells, rod-shaped, spherical, or spiral. Some bacteria cause diseases such as pneumonia, tetanus, and typhoid fever; others do useful things, such as turning cider into vinegar. [**Bacteria** is the plural of **bacterium,** which comes from a Greek word meaning "little rod." Scientists who discovered bacteria saw mostly the rod-shaped kind and named them after their shape.]

bal·co·ny (bal′kə nē), *n.* **1.** an outside platform enclosed by a railing that juts out from an upper floor of a building. **2.** upper floor in a theater, hall, or church that sticks partway over the other floor; gallery. *n., pl.* **bal·co·nies.**

band·wag·on (band′wag′ən), *n.* wagon that carries a musical band in a parade. **climb on the bandwagon,** to join what appears to be a winning or successful group, movement, etc.

bank·rupt·cy (bang′krupt sē), *n.* condition of being unable to pay your debts.

ba·rom·e·ter (bə rom′ə tər), *n.* **1.** device for measuring air pressure, used in determining height above sea level and in predicting probable changes in the weather. **2.** something that indicates changes: *Newspapers are called barometers of public opinion.* [Barometer comes from a Greek word meaning "weight," and the English word *meter,* meaning "device that measures." When air is under more pressure, it weighs more.]

bar·ter (bär′tər), **1.** *v.* to trade by exchanging one kind of goods for other goods without using money; exchange: *barter furs for supplies.* **2.** *n.* trading by exchanging goods. –**bar′ter·er**, *n.*

bat·tal·ion (bə tal′yən), *n.* **1.** military unit made up of two or more companies or batteries, usually commanded by a major or a lieutenant colonel. It is usually part of a group or a regiment. **2.** any large group organized to act together: *A battalion of volunteers helped to rescue the flood victims.*

bi·as (bī′əs), **1.** *n.* tendency to favor or oppose someone or something without real cause; prejudice: *An umpire should have no bias.* **2.** *v.* to influence, usually unfairly; prejudice: *Judges cannot let their feelings bias their decisions. n., pl.* **bi·as·es;** *v.* **bi·ased, bi·as·ing,** or **bi·assed, bi·as·sing.**

bib·li·og·ra·phy (bib′lē og′rə fē), *n.* list of books or articles by a certain author or about a particular subject or person. *n., pl.* **bib·li·og·ra·phies.**

bi·lin·gual (bī ling′gwəl), *adj.* able to speak another language as well or almost as well as your own; knowing two languages.

bi·no·mi·al (bī nō′mē əl), **1.** *n.* expression in algebra containing two terms connected by a plus or minus sign. *8a + 2b is a binomial.* **2.** *adj.* made up of two terms or words. —**bi·no′mi·al·ly,** *adv.*

bi·o·chem·is·try (bī′ō kem′ə strē), *n.* science that deals with the chemical processes of living animals and plants.

bi·o·de·grad·a·ble (bī′ō di grā′də bəl), *adj.* able to be eaten or otherwise broken down by bacteria or other living things: *a biodegradable detergent.* —**bi′o·de·grad′a·bil′i·ty,** *n.*

bi·o·graph·i·cal (bī′ə graf′ə kəl), *adj.* **1.** of someone's life: *biographical details.* **2.** of or about biography. —**bi′o·graph′i·cal·ly,** *adv.*

bi·ome (bī′ōm), *n.* a major ecological system, having its own kind of climate, plants, animals, and other living things. Desert and rain forest are two kinds of biome.

bi·o·sphere (bī′ə sfir), *n.* the region on and surrounding Earth that can support life, including the atmosphere, water, and soil.

bleak (blēk), *adj.* **1.** chilly; cold: *The bleak winter wind made us shiver.* **2.** cheerless and depressing; dismal: *A prisoner's life is bleak.* —**bleak′ly,** *adv.* —**bleak′ness,** *n.*

bound·ar·y (boun′dər ē), *n.* a limiting line or thing; limit; border: *Lake Superior forms part of the boundary between Canada and the United States. n., pl.* **bound·ar·ies.**

brawn·y (brô′nē), *adj.* strong; muscular. *adj.* **brawn·i·er, brawn·i·est.** —**brawn′i·ness,** *n.*

budg·et (buj′it), **1.** *n.* estimate of the amount of money that will probably be received and spent for various purposes in a given time. Governments, companies, schools, families, etc., make budgets. **2.** *v.* to make a plan for spending: *She budgeted her allowance so that she could save some money each week for a new tennis racket. Budget your time.*

bur·ly (bėr′lē), *adj.* big and strong; sturdy: *a burly wrestler. adj.* **bur·li·er, bur·li·est.** —**bur′li·ness,** *n.*

Cc

cal·lig·ra·phy (kə lig′rə fē), *n.* **1.** beautiful handwriting: *Calligraphy is considered an art in China.* **2.** handwriting.

can·did (kan′did), *adj.* **1.** saying openly what you really think or feel; frank and sincere; outspoken: *a candid reply. Please be candid with me.* **2.** fair; impartial: *a candid decision.* **3.** not posed: *a candid photograph of children playing.* —**can′did·ly,** *adv.* —**can′did·ness,** *n.*

can·di·date (kan′də dāt), *n.* person who seeks, or is suggested by others for some office or honor: *There are three candidates for president of the club.* [**Candidate** comes from a Latin word meaning "dressed in white." In ancient Rome, men trying to get elected wore white clothes to show their spotless records.]

can·dor (kan′dər), *n.* honesty in giving your view or opinion: frankness: *She expressed her view with great candor.*

cap·i·tal (kap′ə təl), *n.* city where government of a country, state, or province is located. *Lincoln is the capital of Nebraska.*

cap·i·tal·ism (kap′ə tə liz′əm), *n.* an economic system in which private individuals or groups of individuals own land, factories, and other means of production. They compete with one another, using the hired labor of other persons, to produce goods and services for profit.

ca·pri·cious (kə prish′əs), *adj.* likely to change suddenly without reason; changeable; fickle: *capricious weather.* —**ca·pri′cious·ly,** *adv.* —**ca·pri′cious·ness,** *n.*

cap·tain (kap′tən), *n.* **1.** head of a group; leader or chief: *the captain of a basketball team.* **2.** a military rank.

car·bo·hy·drate (kär′bō hī′drāt), *n.* any of many related substances made from carbon dioxide and water by green plants in sunlight. Carbohydrates are made of carbon, hydrogen, and oxygen. Sugar and starch are carbohydrates.

car·ni·vore (kär′nə vôr), *n.* any animal that feeds chiefly on flesh. Carnivores have large, strong teeth with sharp cutting edges.

cat·a·clysm (kat′ə kliz′əm), *n.* **1.** a great flood, earthquake, or any sudden, violent change in Earth. **2.** any violent change or upheaval: *Atomic warfare between nations would be a cataclysm for the human race.* —**cat·a·clys·mal** (kat′ə kliz′məl) or **cat·a·clys·mic** (kat′ə kliz′mik), *adj.*

cat·a·comb (kat′ə kōm), *n.* an underground network of tunnels used as a burial place with holes dug into the walls in which to place the dead.

catalog|compete

cat·a·log (kat′l òg), **1.** *n.* list of items in some collection. A library has a catalog of its books, arranged in alphabetical order. Some companies print catalogs with pictures and prices of the things they have for sale. **2.** *v.* to make a catalog of; put in a catalog: *to catalog an insect collection.* Also, **cat·a·logue.** *v.* **cat·a·loged, cat·a·log·ing.** —**cat′a·log′er,** *n.*

cat·a·lyst (kat′l ist), *n.* **1.** substance that causes or speeds up a chemical reaction while remaining practically unchanged itself. Enzymes are important catalysts in digestion. **2.** anything that brings about some change or changes without being directly affected itself: *The first successful heart transplant was the catalyst that sparked widespread scientific work in this field.*

ca·tas·tro·phe (kə tas′trə fē), *n.* a sudden, widespread, or extraordinary disaster; great calamity or misfortune. An earthquake, flood, or fire is a catastrophe. —**cat·a·stroph·ic** (kat′ə strof′ik), *adj.* —**cat′a·stroph′i·cal·ly,** *adv.*

cat·a·ton·ic (kat′ə ton′ik), *adj.* being or appearing to be in a kind of stupor in which rigid physical positions are held for a long time.

cav·al·ry (kav′əl rē), *n.* **1.** (earlier) soldiers who fought on horseback. **2.** soldiers who fight from armored vehicles.

cen·tri·fuge (sen′trə fyüj), *n.* machine that turns and separates two substances with different densities, such as cream from milk or bacteria from a fluid, by means of a centrifugal force.

chlo·ro·phyll (klôr′ə fil), *n.* the green coloring matter of plant cells. In the presence of light it makes carbohydrates, such as starch and sugar, from carbon dioxide and water.

chro·mi·um (krō′mē əm), *n.* a grayish, hard, brittle, metallic element that does not rust or become dull easily when exposed to air. Chromium occurs in compounds that are used as plating, as part of stainless steel and other alloys.

chro·mo·some (krō′mə sōm), *n.* any of the rod-shaped chromatin objects that appear in the nucleus of a cell during cell division. Chromosomes contain DNA molecules that carry the genes that determine heredity.

chro·mo·sphere (krō′mə sfir′), *n.* **1.** a red-hot layer of gas around the sun which can be seen only during a total eclipse. **2.** a similar layer around a star.

chron·ic (kron′ik), *adj.* **1.** lasting a long time: *a chronic disease.* **2.** never stopping; constant; habitual: *a chronic tease.* —**chron′i·cal·ly,** *adv.*

chron·i·cle (kron′ə kəl), **1.** *n.* record of events in the order in which they took place; history; story: *Columbus kept a chronicle of his voyages.* **2.** *v.* to write the history of; tell the story of: *Many of the old monks chronicled the Crusades.* *v.* **chron·i·cled, chron·i·cling.** —**chron′i·cler,** *n.*

chron·o·log·i·cal (kron′ə loj′ə kəl), *adj.* arranged in the order in which things happened: *In telling a story a person usually follows chronological order.* —**chron′o·log′i·cal·ly,** *adv.*

chro·nol·o·gy (krə nol′ə jē), *n.* **1.** science of measuring time and determining the proper order and dates of events. **2.** table or list that gives the exact dates of events arranged in the order in which they happened. *n., pl.* **chro·nol·o·gies** for 2.

ci·pher (sī′fər), **1.** *n.* secret writing; code: *Part of his letter is in cipher.* **2.** *v.* to write a message using secret code: *The spy ciphered a report containing the whole plan.*

ci·phered (sī′fərd), *adv.* encoded; written in secret code.

cir·cu·lar (sèr′kyə lər), *adj.* **1.** round like a circle: *The full moon has a circular shape.* **2.** moving in a circle; going around a circle: *A merry-go-round makes a circular trip.*

cir·cum·nav·i·ga·tion (sèr′kəm nav′ə gā′shən), *n.* sailing around: *Magellan was the first sailor to complete a circumnavigation of the globe.*

cog·ni·tion (kog nish′ən), *n.* act or process of knowing.

cog·ni·zant (kog′nə zənt), *adj.* aware: *When the queen became cognizant of the plot against her, she acted swiftly to crush it.*

col·lo·qui·al (kə lō′kwē əl), *adj.* used in common talk; belonging to everyday, familiar talk; informal. Such expressions as *chimp* for *chimpanzee* and *close shave* for *narrow escape* are colloquial. —**col·lo′qui·al·ly,** *adv.*

com·pass (kum′pəs), *n.* **1.** device for showing directions, having a needle that points to the North Magnetic Pole. **2.** tool consisting of two legs hinged together at one end, used for drawing circles and curved lines and for measuring distances.

com·pel (kəm pel′), *v.* **1.** to drive or urge with force; force: *Rain compelled us to stop our ballgame.* **2.** to bring about by force; command: *A policeman can compel obedience to the law.* *v.* **com·pelled, com·pel·ling.** —**com·pel′ling·ly,** *adv.*

com·pen·sate (kom′pən sāt), *v.* **1.** to give something to someone in order to make up for something lost or taken away: *The children mowed our lawn to compensate us for the window they broke playing ball.* **2.** to pay: *The company compensated her for much of her extra work.* *v.* **com·pen·sat·ed, com·pen·sat·ing.**

com·pete (kəm pēt′), *v.* **1.** to try hard to win or gain something wanted by others; be rivals; contend: *She competed against many fine athletes for the gold medal. It is difficult for a small grocery store to compete with a supermarket.* **2.** to take part in a contest: *Will you compete in the final race?* *v.* **com·pet·ed, com·pet·ing.**

com·pla·cent (kəm plā′snt), *adj.* pleased with yourself or what you have; self-satisfied: *The winner's complacent smile annoyed the loser.* **–com·pla′cent·ly,** *adv.*

com·plex (kəm pleks′ or kom′pleks), *adj.* **1.** made up of a number of parts: *A watch is a complex device.* **2.** hard to understand: *The instructions for building the radio were so complex they were hard to follow.* *n., pl.* **com·plex·es. –com·plex′ly,** *adv.* **–com·plex′ness,** *n.*

com·plex·ion (kəm plek′shen), *n.* **1.** color, quality, and general appearance of the skin, particularly of the face. **2.** general appearance of anything; nature; character: *The complexion of the little farm town was changed when two big factories were built nearby.*

com·pli·cate (kom′plə kāt), *v.* **1.** to make hard to understand or settle; mix up; make complex; confuse: *Too many rules complicate a game.* **2.** to make worse or more mixed up: *Headaches can be complicated by eye trouble.* *v.* **com·pli·cat·ed, com·pli·cat·ing.** [**Complicate** comes from a Latin word meaning "to fold together."]

com·ply (kəm plī′), *v.* to act in agreement with a request or a command: *I will comply with their wishes.* *v.* **comp·lied, comp·ly·ing. –com·pli′er.**

com·pul·sor·y (kəm pul′sər ē), *adj.* **1.** compelled; required: *Attendance at school is compulsory for children over seven years old.* **2.** compelling; using force.

con·cave (kon kāv′ or kon′kāv), *adj.* hollow and curved like the inside of a circle or sphere. **–con·cave′ly,** *adv.*

con·cen·trate (kon′sən trāt), *v.* **1.** to bring or come together in one place: *A magnifying glass can concentrate enough sunlight to scorch paper.* **2.** to pay close attention; focus the mind: *He concentrated on his reading so that he would understand the story.*

con·cen·tric (kən sen′trik), *adj.* having the same center.

con·cil·i·a·to·ry (kən sil′ē ə tôr′ē), *adj.* tending to win over, soothe, or reconcile: *Shaking hands after a fight is a conciliatory gesture.*

con·cise (kən sīs′), *adj.* expressing much in few words; brief but full of meaning: *He gave a concise report of the meeting.* **–con·cise′ly,** *adv.* **–con·cise′ness,** *n.*

con·clude (kən klüd′), *v.* **1.** to reach certain decisions or opinions by reasoning; infer: *From its tracks, we concluded that the animal must have been a bear.* **2.** to arrange; settle: *The two countries concluded a trade agreement.* *v.* **con·clud·ed, con·clu·ding. –con·clud′er,** *n.*

con·dense (kən dens′), *v.* **1.** to make or become denser or more compact: *Milk is condensed by removing much of the water from it.* **2.** to change from a gas or vapor to a liquid. If steam touches cold surfaces, it condenses or is condensed into water. *v.* **con·densed, con·dens·ing. –con·den′sa·ble,** *adj.*

cone (kōn), *n.* **1.** a solid object with flat, round base that narrows to a point at the top. **2.** anything shaped like a cone: *an ice-cream cone, the cone of a volcano.*

con·fi·dant (kon′fə dant or kon′fə dänt), *n.* person trusted with your secret or private affairs; close friend.

con·fi·den·tial (kon′fə den′shəl), *adj.* **1.** told or written as a secret: *a confidential report.* **2.** trusted with secrets or private affairs: *a confidential secretary.* **–con′fi·den′ti·al′i·ty,** *n.* **–con′fi·den′tial·ly,** *adv.* [**Confidential** comes from Latin words meaning "with" and "faith." If you tell someone something confidential, you tell it with faith that it will be kept secret.]

con·flu·ence (kon′flü əns), *n.* **1.** act or place of flowing together: *the confluence of two streams to form a river.* **2.** act of coming together of people or things; throng.

con·jec·ture (kən jek′chər), **1.** *n.* conclusion reached by guessing: *Her estimate of the height of that mountain is only conjecture, not fact.* **2.** *v.* to make a conjecture; guess: *Weather forecasters often have to conjecture about the next day's weather conditions.* *v.* **con·jec·tured, con·jec·tur·ing.**

con·sec·u·tive (kən sek′yə tiv), *adj.* following one right after another; successive: *Monday, Tuesday, and Wednesday are consecutive days of the week.* **–con·sec′u·tive·ly,** *adv.* **–con·sec′u·tive·ness,** *n.*

con·sent (kən sent′), **1.** *v.* to give approval or permission; agree: *My father would not consent to my staying up past 10 p.m.* **2.** *n.* agreement; approval; permission: *We have mother's consent to go swimming.*

con·sist·ent (kən sis′tənt), *adj.* **1.** thinking or acting today in agreement with what you thought yesterday; keeping to the same principles and habits. **2.** in agreement; in accord: *Driving at high speed on a rainy day is not consistent with safety.* **–con·sist′ent·ly,** *adv.*

con·spire (kən spīr′), *v.* **1.** to plan secretly with others to do something unlawful or wrong; plot: *The spies conspired to steal secret government documents.* **2.** to act together, as if by plan: *All things conspired to make her birthday a happy one.* *v.* **con·spired, con·spir·ing.**

con·tempt (kən tempt′), *n.* **1.** the feeling that a person, act, or thing is shameful and disgraceful; scorn: *feel contempt for a cheat.* **2.** condition of being despised or scorned; disgrace: *The traitor was held in contempt.* **3.** disobedience to or open disrespect for the rules or decisions of a court of law or a lawmaking group. A person can be put in jail for contempt of court.

con·tra·dic·tion (kon′trə dik′shən), *n.* **1.** act of denying what has been said; saying the opposite: *The expert spoke without fear of contradiction by his listeners.* **2.** statement or act that contradicts another; denial. **3.** disagreement.

GLOSSARY

con·va·les·cent (kon′və les′nt), **1.** *adj.* recovering health and strength after illness. **2.** *adj.* of or for recovering after illness: *a convalescent home.* **3.** *n.* person recovering after illness.

con·vex (kon veks′ *or* kon′veks), *adj.* curved out like the outside of a circle or sphere; curving out: *The lens of a car headlight is convex on the outside.* **–con·vex′ly,** *adv.*

co·or·di·nate (kō ôrd′n it), *n.* any of a set of numbers that give the position of a point by reference to fixed lines; Cartesian coordinates.

co·ord·i·nate plane (kō ôrd′n it plān), *n.* a grid composed of a horizontal number line (x-axis) and vertical number line (y-axis) upon which coordinates can be plotted.

core (kôr), *n.* **1.** the central or most important part: *The core of her argument against the plan is its costliness.* **2.** the central or innermost part of Earth lying below the mantle.

cor·po·ra·tion (kôr′pə rā′shən), *n.* group of persons who obtain a charter giving them as a group the right to buy and sell, own property, manufacture and ship products, etc., as if it were one person.

corp·u·lent (kôr′pyə lənt), *adj.* large or bulky in body size; fat.

cor·pus·cle (kôr′pus′əl), *n.* any of the cells that form a large part of the blood and lymph. Red corpuscles carry oxygen to the tissues and remove carbon dioxide; some white corpuscles destroy disease germs.

cor·re·la·tion (kôr′ə lā′shən), *n.* **1.** the mutual relation of two or more things: *the correlation between annual rainfall and crop yield.* **2.** act or process of correlating. **–cor′re·la′tion·al,** *adj.*

cou·pon (kü′pon), *n.* **1.** a small piece of paper or part of a package or an advertisement that gives the person who holds it certain rights: *If she saves the coupons that come with each box of soap, she can get a free camera.* **2.** a printed statement of interest due on a bond, which can be cut from the bond and presented for payment. [**Coupon** comes from a French word meaning "to cut." People cut coupons from newspapers, magazines, or packages to get lower prices. Originally, coupons were cut off bonds and turned in for money.]

cra·ter (krā′tər), *n.* **1.** a bowl-shaped hole around the opening of a volcano. **2.** a bowl-shaped hole on the surface of Earth, the moon, etc.: *The meteorite crashed to Earth, forming a huge crater.* **–cra′ter·like′,** *adj.*

cre·den·tial (kri den′shəl), *n.* letter of introduction; reference: *The new ambassador from England presented his credentials to the President.*

cred·i·ble (kred′ə bəl), *adj.* worthy of belief; believable: *Her excuse for being absent was hardly credible.* **–cred′i·bil′i·ty,** *n.* **–cred′i·ble·ness,** *n.* **–cred′i·bly,** *adv.*

cred·it (kred′it), *n.* **1.** honor; praise: *The person who does the work should get the credit.* **2.** person or thing that brings honor or praise: *A brilliant swimmer, she's a credit to her team.*

cres·cent (kres′nt), **1.** *n.* shape of the moon in its first or last quarter. **2.** *adj.* shaped like the moon in its first or last quarter: *a crescent pin.*

crust (krust), **1.** *n.* any hard outside covering: *The frozen crust on the snow was thick enough for us to walk on.* **2.** *n.* the solid outside part of Earth: *Heat below the crust of Earth causes volcanoes to form.* **–crust′like′,** *adj.*

cu·ne·i·form (kyü nē′ə fôrm), **1.** *n.* the wedge-shaped characters used in the writing of ancient Babylonia, Assyria, Persia, etc. **2.** *adj.* composed of cuneiform inscriptions: *cuneiform tablets.*

cur·ren·cy (kėr′ən sē), *n.* money in actual use in a country: *Coins and paper money are currency in the United States. n., pl.* **cur·ren·cies.**

Dd

deb·it (deb′it), **1.** *n.* entry of something owed in an account. **2.** *v.* to charge with or as a debt: *The bank debited her account $500.*

dec·a·dent (dek′ə dənt), **1.** *adj.* falling off; growing worse; declining; decaying: *a decadent nation.* **2.** *n.* a decadent person. **–dec′a·dent·ly,** *adv.*

de·cap·i·tate (di kap′ə tāt), *v.* to cut off the head of; behead. *v.* **de·cap·i·tat·ed, de·cap·i·tat·ing. –de·cap′i·ta′tion,** *n.*

de·cen·tral·ize (dē sen′trə līz), *v.* **1.** to spread or distribute authority, power, etc., among more groups or local governments. **2.** to spread an organization or activity away from a central location, such as a city: *decentralize industry to the suburbs. v.* **de·cen·tral·ized, de·cen·tral·iz·ing. –de·cen′tral·i·za′tion,** *n.*

de·ci·pher·ment (di sī′fər mənt), *n.* the act or process of determining the meaning of something: *the decipherment of the puzzle was very difficult.*

de·fault (di fôlt′), **1.** *n.* failure to do something or to appear somewhere when due; neglect. If, in any contest, one side does not appear, it loses by default. **2.** *v.* to fail to do something or appear somewhere when due: *They defaulted in the tennis tournament. She defaulted on her car payment.*

de·ject·ed (di jek′tid), *adj.* in low spirits; sad; discouraged: *I was feeling dejected and unhappy until I heard the good news.* **–de·ject′ed·ly,** *adv.* **–de·ject·ed·ness,** *n.*

del·uge (del′yüj), *n.* **1.** a great flood: *After the dam broke, the deluge washed away the bridge.* **2.** a heavy fall of rain: *We were caught in a deluge on the way home.*

dem·a·gogue (dem′ə gog), *n.* a popular leader who stirs up the people by appealing to their emotions and prejudices.

de·mo·graph·ics (dem′ə graf′iks), *n.* **1.** *sing.* the study of human populations, especially their ages, spending habits, political preferences, etc. **2.** *pl.* data from a demographic study: *The demographics of the Sunbelt states have changed drastically since 1950.*

de·pend·a·ble (di pen′də bəl), *adj.* reliable; trustworthy: *a dependable person.* —**de·pend′a·bil′i·ty,** *n.* —**de·pend′a·bly,** *adv.*

de·pend·ent var·i·a·ble (di pen′dənt vâr′ē bəl), *n.* a variable in a mathematical equation or expression that changes in response to an independent variable. A dependent variable's value is determined by its relationship to an independent variable.

de·ride (di rid′), *v.* to make fun of; laugh at: *They derided me for my fear of the dark.* *v.* **de·rid·ed, de·rid·ing.** —**de·rid′er,** *n.* —**de·rid′ing·ly,** *adv.*

de·ri·sion (di rizh′ən), *n.* laughter; ridicule: *Their derision hurt my feelings.*

de·ri·sive (di rī′siv), *adj.* showing ridicule; mocking. —**de·ri′sive·ly,** *adv.* —**de·ri′sive·ness,** *n.*

des·o·late (des′ə lit), *adj.* **1.** dreary; dismal: *desolate slums.* **2.** not lived in; deserted: *a desolate house.*

de·spond·ent (di spon′dənt), *adj.* having lost heart, courage, or hope; discouraged; dejected. —**de·spond′ent·ly,** *adv.*

de·tain (di tān′), *v.* **1.** to keep from going ahead; hold back; delay: *The heavy traffic detained us for almost an hour.* **2.** to keep in custody; hold as a prisoner: *The police detained the suspected burglar for further questioning.* —**de·tain′ment,** *n.*

de·vel·op·ment (di vel′əp mənt), *n.* **1.** process of developing; growth: *We watched the development of the seeds into plants.* **2.** group of similar houses or apartment buildings built in one area and usually by the same builder. —**de·vel′op·men′tal,** *adj.* —**de·vel′op·men′tal·ly,** *adv.*

de·vi·a·tion (dē′vē ā′shən), *n.* **1.** act of turning aside from a way, course, rule, truth, etc.: *deviation from your usual schedule, a deviation in the needle of a compass.* **2.** (in statistics) amount of difference between the average of a set of numbers and one number in the set. This amount is used to measure difference from a normal condition.

di·am·e·ter (di am′ə tər), *n.* **1.** a line segment passing from one side through the center of a circle, sphere, etc., to the other side. **2.** the length of such a line segment; measurement from one side to the other through the center; width; thickness: *The diameter of Earth is about 8000 miles.*

dif·fi·dent (dif′ə dənt), *adj.* lacking in self-confidence; shy. —**dif′fi·dent·ly,** *adv.*

di·lu·tion (də lü′shən *or* dī lü′shən), *n.* **1.** act of diluting or condition of being diluted. **2.** something diluted.

di·min·u·tive (də min′yə tiv), **1.** *adj.* very small; tiny; minute: *The dollhouse contained diminutive furniture.* **2.** *n.* word or part of a word that expresses the idea of smallness. The endings *-kin, -let, -ette,* and *-ling* are diminutives. —**di·min′u·tive·ly,** *adv.* —**di·min′u·tive·ness,** *n.*

dis·pel (dis pel′), *v.* to drive away; get rid of: *He helped dispel our fears by explaining what had actually happened.* *v.* **dis·pelled, dis·pel·ling.**

dis·sent (di sent′), **1.** *v.* to differ in opinion; disagree: *Two of the judges dissented from the decision of the other three.* **2.** *n.* difference of opinion; disagreement: *Dissent among the members broke up the club meeting.*

dis·sent·er (di sen′tər), *n.* person who offers a different opinion or disagrees.

dis·so·nance (dis′n əns), *n.* **1.** harshness and unpleasantness of sound; discord. **2.** lack of harmony; disagreement.

dis·tort (dis tôrt′), *v.* **1.** to pull or twist out of shape; change the normal appearance of: *Rage distorted his face.* **2.** to change from the truth; misrepresent: *The driver distorted the facts of the accident to escape blame.* —**dis·tort′er,** *n.*

do·cent (dō′snt), *n.* **1.** a lecturer at a college or university. **2.** a guide, especially a person who gives tours of a museum.

do·cile (dos′əl), *adj.* easily trained or managed; obedient: *a docile horse, a docile student.* —**do·cil′i·ty,** *n.* —**doc′ile·ly,** *adv.*

doc·trine (dok′trən), *n.* **1.** what is taught as true by a church, nation, or group of persons; belief: *religious doctrine.* **2.** what is taught; teachings. —**doc′tri·nal,** *adj.* —**doc·tri·nal·ly,** *adv.*

do·main (dō mān′), *n.* the set whose members are considered as possible replacements for the variable in a given relation; replacement set.

dom·i·cile (dom′ə sil), *n.* **1.** a dwelling place; house; home. **2.** place of permanent residence. A person may have several residences, but only one legal domicile at a time. *v.* **dom·i·ciled, dom·i·cil·ing.**

dominant|ethnocentric

dom·i·nant (dom′ə nənt), *adj.* **1.** most powerful or influential; controlling; ruling; governing: *She was a dominant figure in local politics.* **2.** rising high above its surroundings; towering over: *Dominant hills sheltered the bay.* —**dom′i·nant·ly**, *adv.*

dot plot, *n.* a graph used to represent data by showing dots placed over a number line. Each dot represents a specific quantity of data or information.

dra·mat·ic (drə mat′ik), *adj.* **1.** like a drama; of or about plays: *a dramatic actor.* **2.** seeming like a play; full of action or feeling; exciting: *the dramatic reunion of a family separated during wartime.* —**dra·mat′i·cal·ly**, *adv.*

dur·a·ble (dùr′ə bəl), *adj.* **1.** able to withstand wear, decay, etc.: *durable fabric.* **2.** lasting a long time: *a durable peace.* —**dur′a·bil′i·ty**, *n.* —**dur′a·ble·ness**, *n.* —**dur′a·bly**, *adv.*

Ee

ec·cen·tric (ek sen′trik), *adj.* **1.** out of the ordinary; not usual; odd; peculiar: *Wearing a fur coat in hot weather is eccentric behavior.* **2.** off center; having its axis set off center: *an eccentric wheel.* —**ec·cen′tri·cal·ly**, *adv.*

e·clipse (i klips′), **1.** *n.* process of complete or partial blocking of light from one heavenly body to another. A **solar eclipse** occurs when the moon passes between the sun and Earth. A **lunar eclipse** occurs when Earth passes between the sun and the moon. **2.** *v.* to cut off or dim the light from; darken. *v.* **e·clipsed, e·clips·ing.**

ec·stat·ic (ek stat′ik), *adj.* very joyful; excited and delighted: *an ecstatic look of pleasure.* —**ec·stat′i·cal·ly**, *adv.*

el·e·va·tion (el′ə vā′shən), *n.* **1.** height above Earth's surface: *The airplane flew at an elevation of 20,000 feet.* **2.** height above sea level: *The elevation of Denver is 5280 feet.*

el·lip·sis (i lip′sis), *n.* **1.** marks (... or ***) used to show an omission in writing or printing. **2.** omission of a word or phrase needed to complete a sentence grammatically, but not needed to understand its meaning. EXAMPLE: "She is as tall as her brother" instead of "She is as tall as her brother is tall." *n., pl.* **el·lip·ses** (i lip′sēz′).

el·o·cu·tion (el′ə kyü′shən), *n.* art of speaking or reading clearly and effectively in public.

el·o·quent (el′ə kwənt), *adj.* **1.** having the power of expressing feelings or thoughts with grace and force; having eloquence: *an eloquent speaker.* **2.** very expressive: *eloquent eyes.* —**el′o·quent·ly**, *adv.*

em·pa·thize (em′pə thīz), *v.* to feel empathy: *I empathize with his fear of strange dogs.* *v.* **em·pa·thized, em·pa·thiz·ing.**

em·phat·ic (em fat′ik), *adj.* **1.** said or done with force; strongly expressed: *Her answer was an emphatic "No!"* **2.** attracting attention; very noticeable; striking: *The club made an emphatic success of its party.* —**em·phat′i·cal·ly**, *adv.*

en·ci·pher (en sī′fər), *v.* put a message, etc., into cipher.

en·dem·ic (en dem′ik), *adj.* regularly found among a particular people or in a particular locality: *Cholera is endemic in India.* —**en·dem′i·cal·ly**, *adv.*

en·dorse (en dôrs′), *v.* **1.** to write your name on the back of a check, note, or other document: *She had to endorse the check before the bank would cash it.* **2.** to approve; support: *Parents endorsed the plan for a school playground.* *v.* **en·dorsed, en·dors·ing.** [**Endorse** comes from Latin words meaning "on the back." Celebrities who endorse a product or a project give it their backing.] —**en·dors′er**, *n.*

en·dorse·ment (en dôrs′mənt), *n.* **1.** person's name or other writing on the back of a check, bill, or other document. **2.** approval; support: *endorsement from the dental association.*

en·dure (en dùr′), *v.* **1.** to keep on; last: *Metal and stone endure for a long time.* **2.** to put up with; bear; stand: *The pioneers endured many hardships.* *v.* **en·dured, en·dur·ing.** [**Endure** comes from a Latin word meaning "to make hard." Hard things usually last longer and stand more use than soft things.] —**en·dur′a·ble**, *adj.* —**en·dur′a·bly**, *adv.*

ep·i·dem·ic (ep′ə dem′ik), **1.** *n.* the rapid spread of a disease so that many people have it at the same time: *an epidemic of measles.* **2.** *adj.* affecting many people at the same time; widespread: *The flu became epidemic last winter.* —**ep′i·dem′i·cal·ly**, *adv.* [**Epidemic** comes from Greek words meaning "among" and "people." During an epidemic, disease is widespread, and anyone can catch it.]

ep·i·de·mi·ol·o·gy (ep′ə dē′mē ol′ə jē), *n.* branch of medicine dealing with causes, pattern, prevention, and control of the spread of diseases in a community. —**ep′i·de′mi·o·log′i·cal**, *adj.* —**ep′i·de′mi·ol′o·gist**, *n.*

ep·i·logue or **epilog** (ep′ə lòg), *n.* **1.** a part added after the end of a novel, poem, etc. **2.** speech or poem at the end of a play. It is spoken to the audience by one of the actors.

e·qui·nox (ē′kwə noks), *n.* either of the two times in the year when day and night are of equal length everywhere on Earth. An equinox occurs when the sun passes directly above Earth's equator about March 21 (**vernal equinox**) and about September 23 (**autumnal equinox**), *n., pl.* **e·qui·nox·es.**

eth·no·cen·tric (eth′nō sen′trik), *adj.* characterized by ethnocentrism, or a practice of regarding one's own race or culture as superior to others.

e·vac·u·ate (i vak′yü āt), *v.* **1.** to leave empty; withdraw from: *The tenants evacuated the burning apartment house.* **2.** to withdraw; remove: *Efforts were made to evacuate all civilians from the war zone.* *v.* **e·vac·u·at·ed, e·vac·u·at·ing.** **–e·vac·u·a′tion,** *n.*

e·val·u·a·tion (i val′yü ā′shən), *n.* **1.** act of evaluating: *The jury began its careful evaluation of the evidence.* **2.** appraisal or estimation of the quality, importance, value, or progress of your work: *a year-end evaluation.*

ex·ag·ge·ra·tion (eg zaj′ə rā′shən), *n.* **1.** an exaggerated, or said to be larger or bigger than it is, statement: *It is an exaggeration to say that you would rather die than touch a snake.* **2.** act of exaggerating: *His constant exaggeration made people distrust him.*

ex·ca·vate (ek′skə vāt), *v.* **1.** to make hollow; hollow out; *The tunnel was made by excavating the side of a mountain.* **2.** to make by digging; dig: *The workers excavated a tunnel for the new subway.* *v.* **ex·ca·vat·ed, ex·ca·vat·ing.**

ex·cerpt (ek′sėrpt′ *for noun;* ek sėrpt′ *for verb*), **1.** *n.* passage taken out of a book, etc.; quotation; extract: *The English teacher read the class excerpts from several plays.* **2.** *v.* to take out passages from a book, etc.; quote: *In his report on Eleanor Roosevelt, he included some passages excerpted from her speeches.*

ex·cise (ek sīz′), *v.* to cut out; remove: *The doctor excised some scar tissue.* *v.* **ex·cised, ex·cis·ing. –ex·ci·sion** (ek sizh′ən), *n.*

ex·clu·sive (ek sklü′siv), *adj.* **1.** not divided or shared with others; single; sole: *exclusive rights to sell a product.* **2.** very particular about choosing friends, members, etc.: *It is hard to get admitted to an exclusive club.* **–ex·clu′sive·ly,** *adv.* **–ex·clu′sive·ness,** *n.*

ex·er·cise (ek′sər sīz), **1.** *n.* the active use of the body or mind for its improvement: *Physical exercise is good for the health.* **2.** *v.* to give exercise to; train: *She exercises her horse after school every day.* *v.* **ex·er·cised, ex·er·cis·ing. –ex′er·cis·a·ble,** *adj.* **–ex′er·cis·er,** *n.*

ex·pa·tri·ate (ek spā′trē āt), *v.* **1.** to force someone to leave that person's own country; banish. **2.** to withdraw from your country or citizenship: *Some Americans expatriate themselves and live in Europe.* *v.* **ex·pa·tri·at·ed, ex·pa·tri·at·ing. –ex·pa′tri·a′tion,** *n.*

ex·pend·a·ble (ek spen′də bəl), *adj.* **1.** able to be expended or used up. **2.** worth giving up or sacrificing, especially in order to succeed at a plan. **–ex·pend′a·bil′i·ty,** *n.*

ex·pire (ek spīr′), *v.* **1.** to come to an end of effectiveness: *Your library card has expired.* **2.** to die. *v.* **ex·pired, ex·pir·ing. –ex·pir′er,** *n.*

ex·plic·it (ek splis′it), *adj.* clearly expressed; distinctly stated; definite: *She gave such explicit directions that everyone understood them.* **–ex·plic′it·ly,** *adv.* **–ex·plic′it·ness,** *n.*

ex·pres·sion (ek spresh′ən), *n.* any combination of constants, variables, and symbols expressing some mathematical operation or quantity.

ex·pul·sion (ek spul′shən), *n.* **1.** act of forcing out: *expulsion of air from the lungs.* **2.** condition of being forced out: *expulsion from school for bad behavior.*

ex·tort (ek stôrt′), *v.* to obtain money, a promise, etc., by threats, force, fraud, or wrong use of authority: *Blackmailers try to extort money from their victims.* **–ex·tort′er,** *n.*

ex·trap·o·la·tion (ek strap′ə lā shən), *n.* the act or process of calculating or inferring from what is known something that is possible but unknown; predict from facts.

ex·ub·er·ance (eg zü′bər əns), *n.* **1.** a great abundance: *an exuberance of joy.* **2.** high spirits.

ex·ult·ant·ly (eg zult′nt′lē), *adv.* rejoicing greatly or triumphantly.

Ff

fac·tu·al (fak′chü əl), *adj.* concerned with fact; containing facts: *I wrote a factual account of the field trip for the school newspaper.* **–fac′tu·al·ly,** *adv.*

fal·la·cy (fal′ə sē), *n.* **1.** a false idea; mistaken belief; error: *It is a fallacy that riches always bring happiness.* **2.** mistake in reasoning; misleading or unsound argument. *n., pl.* **fal·la·cies.**

fi·del·i·ty (fi del′ə tē *or* fə del′ə tē), *n.* **1.** steadfast faithfulness; loyalty: *a dog's fidelity to its owner.* **2.** exactness; accuracy: *She repeated the message with absolute fidelity.*

fil·i·bus·ter (fil′ə bus′tər), **1.** *n.* the deliberate hindering of the passage of a bill in a legislature by long speeches or other means of delay. **2.** *v.* to deliberately hinder the passage of a bill by such means. **–fil′i·bus′ter·er,** *n.*

fluc·tu·ate (fluk′chü āt), *v.* to rise and fall; change continually; waver: *The temperature fluctuates from day to day.* *v.* **fluc·tu·at·ed, fluc·tu·at·ing. –fluc′tu·a′tion,** *n.*

flu·ent (flü′ənt), *adj.* **1.** flowing smoothly or easily: *to speak fluent French.* **2.** speaking or writing easily or rapidly: *She is a fluent lecturer.* **–flu′ent·ly,** *adv.*

foot·note (fút′nōt′), *n.* note at the bottom of a page about something on the page.

fore·bode (fôr bōd′), *v.* to give warning of; predict: *Those black clouds forebode a storm.* *v.* **fore·bod·ed, fore·bod·ing.**

GLOSSARY

fore·go (fôr gō′), v. to do without; give up: *She decided to forego the movies and do her lessons.* v. **fore·went, fore·gone, fore·go·ing. –fore·go′er,** n.

fore·sight (fôr′sīt), n. **1.** ability to see what is likely to happen and prepare for it: *No one had enough foresight to predict the winner.* **2.** careful thought about what is likely to happen in the future; prudence: *A spendthrift does not use foresight.*

fore·warn (fôr wôrn′), v. to warn beforehand: *We should have been forewarned of his illness when he began to lose weight.*

for·lorn (fôr lôrn′), adj. miserable and hopeless from being left alone and neglected: *the lost kitten, a forlorn little animal, was wet and dirty.* **–for·lorn′ly,** adv. **–for·lorn′ness,** n.

fra·ter·nal (frə tèr′nl), adj. **1.** of brothers or a brother; brotherly. **2.** of or about a group organized for mutual fellowship: *a fraternal association.* **–fra·ter′nal·ly,** adv.

frat·er·ni·za·tion (frat′ər nə zā shən), v. the act of associating in a brotherly way; being friendly.

frat·er·nize (frat′ər nīz), v. to associate in a brotherly way; be friendly. v. **frat·er·nized, frat·er·niz·ing, -frat′er·ni·za′tion,** n. **–frat′er·niz′er,** n.

fresh·wa·ter (fresh′wȯ′tər), adj. of or living in water that is not salty: *a freshwater fish.*

func·tion (fungk′shən) n. **1.** proper work; normal action or use; purpose: *The function of the stomach is to help digest food.* **2.** (in mathematics) **a.** a quantity whose value depends on the value given to another related quantity: *The area of a circle is a function of its radius.* **b.** a relationship between two sets such that each element in the first set is associated with exactly one element in the second set. **–func′tion·less,** adj.

Gg

gal·lant (gal′ənt), adj. **1.** noble in sprit or in conduct; brave: *She was praised for her gallant action in saving the drowning child.* **2.** very polite and attentive to women. **–gal′lant·ly,** adv. **–gal′lant·ness,** n.

gar·ri·son (gar′ə sən), **1.** n. group of soldiers stationed in a fort, town, etc., to defend it. **2.** v. to station soldiers in a fort, town, etc., to defend it.

gen·er·al·i·za·tion (jen′ər ə lə zā′shən), n. a general idea, statement, principle, or rule: *"A rainbow appears when the sun shines after a shower" is a generalization.*

ge·o·ther·mal (jē′ō thèr′məl), adj. of or produced by the internal heat of Earth: *geothermal energy.*

gov·ern·ment (guv′ərn mənt), n. **1.** person or persons ruling a country, state, district, etc., at any time. The government of the United States consists of the President, the cabinet, and administrative assistants appointed by the President. **2.** system of ruling: *The United States has a democratic form of government.* **–gov′ern·men′tal,** adj. **–gov′ern·men′tal·ly,** adv.

gram·mar·ian (grə mer′ē ən), n. an expert in grammar.

gram·mat·i·cal (grə mat′ə kəl), adj. **1.** according to the rules of grammar: *Our French teacher speaks grammatical English, but has a French accent.* **2.** of grammar: *"You should have saw it" is a grammatical mistake.* **–gram·mat′i·cal·ly,** adv. **–gram·mat′i·cal·ness,** n.

graph·ite (graf′īt), n. a soft, black form of carbon used for pencil leads and for greasing machinery.

ground wa·ter (ground′ wȯ′tər), n. water that flows or seeps downward, saturates the rock below the soil, and supplies springs and wells.

Hh

her·bi·cide (hèr′bə sīd *or* èr′bə sīd), n. a poisonous chemical used to destroy weeds.

her·bi·vore (èr′bə vôr *or* hèr′bə vôr), n. any animal that feeds mainly on plants.

hi·er·o·glyph·ic (hī′ər ə glif′ik), n. **1.** picture, character, or symbol standing for a word, idea, or sound. The ancient Egyptians used hieroglyphics instead of an alphabet like ours. **2. hieroglyphics,** pl. writing that uses hieroglyphics. **–hi′er·o·glyph′i·cal·ly,** adv. [**Hieroglyphic** comes from a Greek word meaning "sacred carving." Greeks believed hieroglyphics were a secret writing that only priests could read.]

hin·ter·land (hin′tər land′), n. **1.** land or district behind a coast. **2.** region far from towns or cities; thinly settled country.

hol·o·gram (hol′ə gram *or* hō′lə gram), n. a kind of photograph showing three dimensions. A hologram is made by exposing film to two sources of light. One source is a laser beam and the other is light reflected from an object lit by the same laser beam. To view a hologram, light is passed through the film, and an image of the object appears, apparently solid.

hom·i·cide (hom′ə sīd), n. **1.** act of killing one human being by another. **2.** person who kills another human being.

hy·drate (hī′drāt), **1.** n. any chemical compound made when certain substances chemically unite with water. **2.** v. to become or cause to become a hydrate; combine with water to form a hydrate. v. **hy·drat·ed, hy·drat·ing, –hy·dra′tion,** n.

hy·drau·lic (hī drȯ′lik), *adj.* **1.** of or about hydraulics. **2.** operated by the pressure of water or other liquids in motion: *a hydraulic press.*

hy·dro·e·lec·tric (hī′drə i lek′trik), *adj.* producing electricity by using the power of moving water.

hy·drol·o·gy (hī drol′ə jē), *n.* science that deals with water and its properties, laws, geographical distribution, etc.

hy·dro·plane (hī′drə plān), *n.* **1.** a fast motorboat that glides on the surface of water. **2.** seaplane.

hy·dro·sphere (hī′drə sfir), *n.* water on the surface of Earth, sometimes also thought of as including the water vapor in the atmosphere.

hy·per·bo·la (hi pėr′bə lə), *n.* a curve formed when a cone is cut by a plane that is closer to the vertical than the side of the cone is. *n., pl.* **hy·per·bo·las.**

hy·per·bo·le (hī pėr′bə lē), *n.* an exaggerated statement used for effect and not meant to be taken literally, such as "I'm so hungry I could eat a horse."

Ii

i·de·al·ism (ī dē′ə liz′əm), *n.* **1.** practice of acting according to your ideals of what ought to be, regardless of what happens or of what other people may think; a cherishing of fine ideals. **2.** act of neglecting practical matters in following ideals; not being practical.

id·i·om (id′ē əm), *n.* phrase or expression whose meaning cannot be understood from the ordinary meaning of the words in it. "Hold your tongue" is an English idiom meaning "keep quiet."

il·le·git·i·mate (il′i jit′ə mit), *adj.* **1.** not according to the law or the rules. **2.** born of parents who are not married to each other. –**il′le·git′i·mate·ly,** *adv.*

il·log·i·cal (i loj′ə kəl), *adj.* **1.** contrary to the principles of sound reasoning; not logical: *Your illogical behavior worries me.* **2.** not reasonable; foolish: *an illogical fear of the dark.* –**il·log′i·cal·ly,** *adv.* –**il·log′i·cal·ness,** *n.*

im·men·si·ty (i men′sə tē), *n.* very great size or extent; vastness: *the ocean's immensity.*

im·plic·it (im plis′it), *adj.* **1.** meant, but not clearly expressed; implied: *Her opposition to the present tax laws was implicit in her speech on tax reform.* **2.** without doubting, hesitating, or asking questions; absolute: *He had implicit confidence in his friend.* **im·plic′it·ly,** *adv.* –**im·plic′it·ness,** *n.*

im·ply (im plī′), *v.* to mean without saying so; express indirectly; suggest: *The teacher's smile implied that she had forgiven us.* *v.* **im·plied, im·ply·ing.** [**Imply** comes from the Latin word meaning "to fold in." An implied meaning is folded into words or actions.]

im·pulse (im′puls), *n.* **1.** a sudden inclination or urge: *I had a strong impulse to contact my old friend.* **2.** a sudden, driving force or influence; thrust; push: *the impulse of hunger, the impulse of curiosity.*

in·can·des·cent (in′kən des′nt), *adj.* **1.** glowing with heat; red-hot or white-hot: *Steel comes from the furnace as an incandescent liquid.* **2.** shining brightly; brilliant. –**in′can·des′cent·ly,** *adv.*

in·ci·sion (in sizh′ən), *n.* **1.** a cut made into something, especially surgically. **2.** act of incising.

in·clu·sion (in klü′zhən), *n.* **1.** act of including or condition of being included. **2.** something included.

in·cog·ni·to (in′kog nē′tō *or* in kog′nə tō), *adj., adv.* with your real name, character, rank, etc., hidden: *A disguise allows you to be incognito. The prince traveled incognito to avoid crowds and ceremonies.* [**Incognito** comes from Latin words meaning "not to get to know." The reason for being incognito is so that people don't get to know the truth.]

in·con·clu·sive (in′kən klü′siv), *adj.* not convincing; not settling or deciding something doubtful; not effective: *The result of my blood test was inconclusive, so I'll have to have another test.* **in′con·clu′sive·ly,** *adv.* –**in′conclu′sive·ness,** *n.*

in·cor·po·rate (in kôr′pə rāt), *v.* **1.** to make something a part of something else; join or combine something with something else: *We will incorporate your suggestion in this new plan.* **2.** to make into a corporation: *When the business became large, the owners incorporated it.* *v.* **in·cor·po·rat·ed, in·cor·po·rat·ing.** –**in·cor′po·ra′tion,** *n.* [**Incorporate** comes from Latin words meaning "into a body." In business, people incorporate by forming a group that has the legal right to operate a company, as if the group were a single person.]

in·cred·u·lous (in krej′ə ləs), *adj.* **1.** not ready to believe; doubting: *Most people nowadays are incredulous about ghosts and witches.* **2.** showing a lack of belief: *He listened to the neighbor's story with an incredulous smile.* **in·cred′u·lous·ly,** *adv.*

in·de·ci·pher·a·ble (in′di sī′fər ə bəl), *adj.* not able to be deciphered; impossible to read: *Her handwriting is indecipherable.*

in·de·pend·ent var·i·a·ble (in di pen′dənt vâr′ē ə bəl), *n.* a variable in a mathematical expression whose value does not depend on the value of another variable.

in·dis·pen·sa·ble (in′dis pen′sə bəl), *adj.* absolutely necessary: *Air is indispensable to life.* –**in′dis·pen′sa·bil′i·ty, in′dis·pen′sa·ble·ness,** *n.* –**in′dis·pen′sa·bly,** *adv.*

in·doc·tri·nate (in dok′trə nāt), *v.* **1.** to teach a particular belief or doctrine so that it is accepted uncritically. **2.** to teach; instruct. *v.* **in·doc·tri·nat·ed, in·doc·tri·nat·ing,** –**in·doc′tri·na′tion,** *n.* –**in·doc′tri·na′tor,** *n.*

GLOSSARY

in·fan·try (in′fən trē), *n.* **1.** soldiers trained, equipped, and organized to fight on foot. **2.** branch of an army consisting of such troops. [**Infantry** comes from Latin words meaning "not" and "speak." **Infant** comes from the same words. An infant to too young to speak. In old times, many foot soldiers were boys too young to be made knights. They were called "infants," perhaps as a joke. The name stuck, even when most infantry were full-grown men.]

in·fi·del (in′fə dəl), **1.** *n.* person who does not believe in religion. **2.** *adj.* not believing in religion.

in·fla·tion (in flā′shən), *n.* **1.** a sharp or steady increase in prices of goods. **2.** a swollen state; too great expansion.

in·flec·tion (in flek′shən), *n.* **1.** a change in the tone or pitch of the voice: *We usually end questions with a rising inflection.* **2.** variation in the form of a word to show case, number, gender, person, tense, mood, voice, or comparison. **3.** suffix or ending used for this: *-est and -ed are common inflections in English.*

in·flu·ence (in′flü əns), *n.* **1.** power of acting on others and having an effect without using force: *Use your influence to persuade your friends to join our club.* **2.** person or thing that has such power: *My older sister was a good influence on me.*

in·ject (in jekt′), *v.* **1.** to force liquid into the body through a hollow needle: *inject penicillin into a muscle.* **2.** to throw in; insert: *While she and I were talking he injected a remark into the conversation.* –**in·ject′a·ble**, *adj.* –**in·jec′tor**, *n.*

in·junc·tion (in jungk′shən), *n.* **1.** a formal order from a court of law requiring a person or group to do or not to do something: *The injunction prohibited the teachers from striking before the end of the school year.* **2.** command; order: *The driver obeyed the police officer's injunction to pull over.*

in·jure (in′jər), *v.* to do damage to; harm; hurt: *I injured my arm while skiing. The misunderstanding injured their relationship.* *v.* **in·jured, in·jur·ing.**

in·spire (in spīr′), *v.* **1.** to fill with a thought or feeling; influence: *A chance to try again inspired her with hope.* **2.** to fill with excitement: *His speech inspired the crowd.* *v.* **in·spired, in·spir·ing.** –**in·spir′a·ble**, *adj.* –**in·spir′er**, *n.* –**in·spir′ing·ly**, *adv.*

in·tact (in takt′), *adj.* with nothing missing or broken; whole; untouched; uninjured: *The missing money was found and returned to the bank intact.* –**in·tact′ness**, *n.*

in·tan·gi·ble (in tan′jə bəl), *adj.* **1.** not capable of being touched or felt: *Sound and light are intangible.* **2.** not easily grasped by the mind; vague: *Charm is an intangible quality.* –**in·tan′gi·bil′i·ty, in·tan′gi·ble·ness**, *n.* –**in·tan′gi·bly**, *adv.*

in·ter·fra·tern·i·ty (in′tər frə tėr′nə tē), *n.* friendly cooperation between two separate groups.

in·ter·sect (in′tər sekt′), *v.* **1.** to cross; cut or divide by passing through or across: *A path intersects the field.* **2.** (in geometry) to have one or more points in common: *intersecting circles.*

in·va·lid (in′və lid), **1.** *n.* person who is weak because of sickness or injury. An invalid cannot get around and do things. **2.** *adj.* weak because of sickness or injury; not well; disabled.

i·so·late (ī′sə lāt), *v.* to separate from others; keep alone: *A storm washed out the bridge, isolating the island from the mainland.* *v.* **i·so·lat·ed, i·so·lat·ing.** [**Isolate** comes from a Latin word meaning "island." If you're isolated, you're cut off from others, like an island.]

isth·mus (is′məs), *n.* a narrow strip of land with water on both sides connecting two larger bodies of land: *The Isthmus of Panama connects North America and South America.* *n., pl.* **isth·mus·es.**

Jj

jar·gon (jär′gən), *n.* language of a special group, profession, etc. Doctors, actors, and sailors have jargons.

jub·i·la·tion (jü′bə lā′shən), *n.* great joy.

ju·di·cial (jü dish′əl), *adj.* **1.** of or by judges; of or about courts or the administration of justice: *The judicial branch of government enforces the laws.* **2.** of or suitable for a judge; impartial; fair: *a judicial mind.* –**ju·di′cial·ly**, *adv.*

ju·di·cious (jü dish′əs), *adj.* having, using, or showing good judgment; wise; sensible: *Judicious parents encourage their children to make their own decisions.* –**ju·di′cious·ly**, *adv.* –**ju·di′cious·ness**, *n.*

junc·tion (jungk′shən), *n.* **1.** place of joining or meeting. A railroad junction is a place where railroad lines meet or cross. **2.** act of joining or the condition of being joined: *The junction of the two rivers results in a large flow of water downstream.*

junc·ture (jungk′chər), *n.* **1.** point of time, especially a critical time or state of affairs: *At this juncture we must decide what move to make next.* **2.** point or line where two things join; joint.

jur·is·dic·tion (jur′is dik′shən), *n.* **1.** authority; power; control: *The principal has jurisdiction over the teachers in a school.* **2.** territory over which authority extends.

jus·ti·fy (jus′tə fī), *v.* **1.** to give a good reason for: *The fine quality of the cloth justifies its high price.* **2.** to show to be just or right: *Can you justify your act?* *v.* **jus·ti·fied, jus·ti·fy·ing.**

Ll

land·form (land′fôrm′), *n.* physical feature of Earth's surface. Plains, plateaus, hills, and mountains are landforms.

land·mark (land′märk′), *n.* **1.** something familiar or easily seen, used as a guide: *The traveler did not lose her way in the forest because the rangers' high tower served as a landmark.* **2.** a building, monument, or place designated as important or interesting: *That old building is a historical landmark.*

lat·i·tude (lat′ə tüd), *n.* **1.** distance north or south of the equator, measured in degrees. A degree of latitude is about 69 miles (111 kilometers). **2.** place or region having a certain latitude: *Polar bears live in the cold latitudes.* [**Latitude** comes from a Latin word meaning "wide." Roman maps were much wider than they were long, and lines of latitude went across the wide way.]

laun·der (lôn′dər), *v.* **1.** to wash and iron clothes, tablecloths, towels, etc. **2.** to be able to be washed; stand washing: *Cotton materials usually launder well.* –**laun′der·a·ble,** *adj.* –**laun′der·er,** *n.*

la·va (lä′və *or* lav′ə), *n.* **1.** hot, melted rock flowing from a volcano. **2.** rock formed by the cooling of this melted rock. Some lavas are hard and glassy; others are light and porous. *n., pl.* **la·vas.**

lav·a·to·ry (lav′ə tôr′ē), *n.* **1.** bathroom; toilet. **2.** bowl or basin to wash in. *n., pl.* **lav·a·to·ries.**

lav·ish (lav′ish), *adj.* **1.** very free in giving or spending; extravagant: *A very rich person can be lavish with money.* **2.** very abundant; more than is needed: *A lavish helping of dessert.*

le·gal·is·tic (lē′gə lis′tik), *adj.* adhering strictly to law or prescription. –**le′gal·is′ti·cal·ly,** *adv.*

le·gal·ize (lē′gə līze), *v.* to make legal; authorize by law; sanction. *v.* **le·gal·ized, le·gal·iz·ing.** –**le′gal·i·za′tion,** *n.*

leg·is·la·tive (lej′ə slā′tiv), *adj.* **1.** involving the making of laws: *legislative reforms.* **2.** having the duty and power or making laws: *Congress is a legislative group.*

leg·is·la·tor (lej′ə slā′tər), *n.* member of a legislative group; lawmaker. Senators and Representatives are legislators.

leg·is·la·ture (lej′ə slā′chər), *n.* group of persons that has the duty and power of making laws for a state or country.

li·bel (lī′bəl), **1.** *n.* a written or published statement that is likely to harm the reputation of the person about whom it is made; false or damaging statement. **2.** *v.* to write or publish such a statement about. *v.* **li·beled, li·bel·ing** or **li·belled, li·bell·ing.** –**li′bel·er,** *n.*

lin·gui·ne (ling gwē′nē), *n.* kind of pasta similar to spaghetti, cut into long, thin, flat pieces. Linguine is often served with clam sauce.

lin·guist (ling′gwist), *n.* **1.** an expert in languages or linguistics. **2.** person skilled in a number of languages.

lit·er·a·cy (lit′ər ə sē), *n.* **1.** ability to read and write. **2.** having understanding of the essentials of a particular area of knowledge: *computer literacy.*

lit·e·rar·y (lit′ə rer′ē), *adj.* **1.** of or referring to literature. **2.** knowing much about literature.

lit·er·ate (lit′ər it), *adj.* **1.** able to read and write. **2.** having understanding of the essentials of a particular subject: *courses designed to make students literate in science.*

lo·gis·ti·cal·ly (lō jis′ti kə lē), *adv.* of or about the planning and carrying out of any complex or large-scale operation, especially one of military movement, evacuation, and supply.

lon·gi·tude (lon′jə tüd), *n.* distance east or west on Earth's surface, measured in degrees from a certain meridian, usually the one through Greenwich, England. A degree of longitude is about 69 miles (111 kilometers) at the equator.

lo·qua·cious (lō kwā′shəs), *adj.* talking much; fond of talking. –**lo·qua′cious·ly,** *adv.* –**lo·qua′cious·ness,** *n.*

lu·nar (lü′nər), *adj.* **1.** of or like the moon: *a lunar landscape.* **2.** measured by the moon's revolution around Earth: *a lunar month.*

Mm

mag·ma (mag′mə), *n.* the very hot, melted rock beneath Earth's crust from which igneous rock is formed. [**Magma** comes from a Greek word meaning "to squeeze in the hands." Magma oozes and spreads as dough or clay does if you squeeze it.]

mag·ni·tude (mag′nə tüd), *n.* **1.** greatness of size: *The magnitude of destruction caused by the hurricane had to be seen to be believed.* **2.** great importance or effect: *The war brought problems of immense magnitude to many nations.*

main·tain (mān tān′), *v.* **1.** to keep; keep up; carry on: *You must maintain your footing in a tug-of-war.* **2.** to keep supplied, equipped, or in repair: *The company employs people to maintain the machinery.* [**Maintain** comes from Latin words meaning "to hold in the hand." Maintaining something carefully is like carrying it around with you.]

man·tle (man′tl), *n.* the layer of Earth beneath the crust and above the core.

massive|objection

mas·sive (mas′iv), *adj.* **1.** big and heavy; bulky: *a massive boulder.* **2.** great in amount, scale, or effect: *massive doses of medicine, a massive mural, a massive stroke.* —**mas′sive·ly,** *adv.* —**mas′sive·ness,** *n.*

ma·ter·nal (mə tėr′nl), *adj.* **1.** of or like a mother; motherly: *maternal instincts.* **2.** related on the mother's side of the family: *maternal grandparents.* —**ma·ter′nal·ly,** *adv.*

ma·tri·arch (mā′trē ärk), *n.* **1.** mother who is the ruler of a family or tribe. **2.** a highly respected elderly woman. *n., pl.* **ma·tri·archs.**

ma·tri·cide (mat′rə sīd), *n.* **1.** act of killing your mother. **2.** someone who kills his or her mother. —**ma′tri·cid′al,** *adj.*

mat·ri·mo·ny (mat′rə mō′nē), *n.* the condition of being married. —**mat′ri·mo′ni·al,** *adj.* —**mat′ri·mo′ni·al·ly,** *adv.*

ma·trix (mā′triks *or* mat′riks), *n.* something that produces or gives form to something else it surrounds or encloses. A mold for a casting is called a matrix. *n., pl.* **ma·trix·es** *or* **ma·tri·ces.**

mel·an·chol·y (mel′ən kol′ē), **1.** *n.* depression; sadness; tendency to be sad. **2.** *adj.* sad; gloomy: *a melancholy person.*

me·lee (mā′lā), *n.* a confused fight; hand-to-hand fight among a number of fighters. *n., pl.* **me·lees.**

mem·oir (mem′wär), *n.* **1.** biography. **2. memoirs,** *pl.* **a.** record of facts and events written from personal knowledge or special information: *The retired general wrote his memoirs of army life.* **b.** record of someone's own life and experiences; autobiography.

met·ro·nome (met′rə nōm), *n.* device that can be adjusted to make loud ticking sounds at different speeds. Metronomes are used especially to mark time for persons practicing on musical instruments.

me·trop·o·lis (mə trop′ə lis), *n.* **1.** a large city; important center: *Chicago is a busy metropolis.* **2.** the most important city of a country or region: *New York is the metropolis of the United States. n., pl.* **me·trop·o·lis·es.**

mi·cro·graph (mī′krə graf), *n.* magnified image or photograph of an object taken through a microscope.

mi·gra·tion (mī grā′shən), *n.* **1.** act of migrating: *Some kinds of birds travel thousands of miles on their migrations.* **2.** number of people or animals migrating together.

min·e·ral (min′ər əl), *n.* **1.** substance obtained by mining. Coal, gold, and mica are minerals. **2.** any chemical element the body needs to get in small amounts from food in order to function properly, such as calcium, potassium, etc.

mis·con·strue (mis′kən strü′), *v.* to take in a wrong or mistaken sense; misunderstand: *Shyness is sometimes misconstrued as unfriendliness. v.* —**mis·con·strued, mis·con·stru·ing.**

mol·li·fy (mol′ə fī), *v.* to reduce someone else's anger: *I tried to mollify my parents by apologizing for losing my jacket. v.* **mol·li·fied, mol·li·fy·ing.** —**mol′li·fi·ca′tion,** *n.*

mol·ten (mōlt′n), *adj.* **1.** made liquid by heat; melted: *molten steel.* **2.** made by melting and casting: *a molten image.*

mon·o·chro·ma·tic (mon′ə krō mat′ik), *adj.* having or showing one color only.

mon·o·gram (mon′ə gram), *n.* someone's initials combined in one design. Monograms are used on note paper, table linen, clothing, jewelry, etc.

mon·o·graph (mon′ə graf), *n.* book or article, especially a scholarly one, about a particular subject.

mon·o·logue (mon′l òg), *n.* **1.** a long speech by one person in a group. **2.** part of a play in which a single actor speaks alone.

Nn

na·val (nā′vəl), *adj.* **1.** of or for warships or the navy: *a naval officer; naval supplies; naval bases.* **2.** having a navy: *Spain was once a great naval power.*

nav·i·ga·ble (nav′ə gə bəl), *adj.* **1.** able to be traveled by ships: *The river is deep enough to be navigable for hundreds of miles.* **2.** able to be steered: *a navigable balloon.* —**nav′i·ga·bil′i·ty, nav′i·ga·ble·ness,** *n.* —**nav′i·ga·bly,** *adv.*

nav·i·ga·tor (nav′ə gā′tər), *n.* **1.** person in charge of finding the position and course of a ship or aircraft. **2.** (long ago) explorer of the seas.

niche (nich), *n.* **1.** a hollow place made in a wall for a statue, vase, etc., to stand. **2.** (in biology) a usual way of life of a particular species or living thing in an environment or community: *The cat's original niche was as a predator of small animals.*

non se·qui·tur (non sek′wə tər), *n.* inference or conclusion that does not follow from the premises. [**Non sequitur** comes from Latin words meaning "it does not follow."]

Oo

ob·jec·tion (əb jek′shən), *n.* **1.** something said as a reason or argument against something: *One of his objections to the plan was that it would cost too much.* **2.** feeling of disapproval or dislike: *an energetic person with no objection to hard work.*

o·blit·e·rate (ə blit′ə rāt′), v. **1.** to remove all traces of: *The heavy rain obliterated the footprints.* **2.** to destroy completely: *An earthquake obliterated the village.* v. **o·blit·er·at·ed, o·blit·er·at·ing.** –**o·blit′er·a′tion,** n. –**o·blit′er·a′tor,** n.

ob·se·qui·ous (əb sē′kwē əs), adj. overly attentive to someone thought to be important: *Obsequious courtiers greeted the royal couple.* –**ob·se′qui·ous·ly,** adv. –**ob·se′qui·ous·ness,** n.

ob·ser·va·tion (ob′zər vā′shən), n. **1.** act, habit, or power of seeing and noting: *By trained observation a doctor can tell much about the condition of a patient.* **2.** something seen and noted: *During science experiments she kept careful records of her observations.* –**ob′ser·va′tion·al,** adj. –**ob′ser·va′tion·al·ly,** adv.

ob·serv·a·to·ry (əb zėr′və tôr′ē), n. **1.** building equipped with telescopes and other devices for watching and studying astronomical objects. **2.** a high place or building giving a wide view. n., pl. **ob·serv·a·to·ries.**

ob·tuse (əb tüs′), adj. **1.** slow in understanding; stupid: *They were too obtuse to take the hint.* **2.** not sharp or acute; blunt. –**ob·tuse′ly,** adv. –**ob·tuse′ness,** n.

oc·clude (o klüd′), v. **1.** to stop up or block off something that is normally open; obstruct. **2.** to meet closely in proper position. *The teeth in the upper jaw and those in the lower jaw should occlude.* v. **oc·clud·ed, oc·clud·ing.**

om·nis·cient (om nish′ənt), adj. knowing everything; having complete or infinite knowledge. –**om·nis′cient·ly,** adv.

om·ni·vore (om′nə vôr′), n. person or animal that eats all kinds of food.

out·li·er (out′lī′ėr), n. something that lies outside the boundary or the main group.

ox·y·gen (ok′sə jən), n. a colorless, odorless gas that forms about one fifth of the air, and about one third of water. Oxygen is a chemical element present in combined form in water, carbon dioxide, iron ore, and many other substances. Animals and plants cannot live, and fire will not burn, without oxygen.

ox·y·mo·ron (ok′si môr′on), n. a figure of speech in which words of opposite meaning or suggestion are used together. *Burning cold, bittersweet, sad laughter,* and *jumbo shrimp* are oxymorons. [**Oxymoron** comes from Greek words meaning "sharp" and "stupid." An oxymoron looks stupid at first but has a real point.]

Pp

pac·i·fy (pas′ə fī), v. **1.** to make peaceful; quiet down: *pacify angry demonstrators, pacify a crying baby.* **2.** to bring under control; control by force; subdue: *pacify a rebellious region.* v. **pac·i·fied, pac·i·fy·ing.** –**pac′i·fi′a·ble,** adj. –**pac′i·fi·ca′tion,** n.

pal·in·drome (pal′in drōm), n. word, verse, sentence, or number which reads the same backward or forward. *Madam, radar,* "Madam, I'm Adam," and *247742* are palindromes.

pa·py·rus (pə pī′rəs), n. **1.** a tall water plant from which the ancient Egyptians, Greeks, and Romans made a material to write on. **2.** this writing material.

pa·rab·o·la (pə rab′ə lə), n. a curve formed by all the points that are equally distant from a line and a point not on that line. A parabola is also produced by the intersection of a cone and a plane parallel to a side of the cone. The trajectory of a missile is a parabola. n., pl. **pa·rab·ol·as.**

pa·ram·e·ter (pə ram′ə tər), n. **1.** a particular quality; characteristic feature: *The parameters of the pollution problem include population, technology, weather, and other factors.* **2.** a limit or boundary: *as much information as the parameters of an encyclopedia allow.*

par·a·sol (par′ə sòl), n. a light umbrella used as protection from the sun.

parch·ment (pärch′mənt), n. **1.** the skin of sheep or goats, prepared for use as a writing material. **2.** manuscript or document written on parchment. –**parch′ment·like′,** adj.

pa·ren·the·ses (pə ren′thə sēz), n., pl. two curved lines ( ) used to set off a word, phrase, sentence, etc., inserted within a sentence to explain or qualify something.

pa·thet·ic (pə thet′ik), adj. causing pity; pitiful: *The stray dog was a pathetic sight.* –**pa·thet′i·cal·ly,** adv.

path·o·gen (path′ə jən), n. anything capable of producing disease, especially a living microorganism or virus.

path·ol·o·gist (pa thol′ə jist), n. an expert in pathology, or the study of the causes and nature of diseases.

pa·thos (pā′thos), n. quality in speech, writing, music, events, or a scene that causes pity or sadness.

pat·ri·cide (pat′rə sīd), n. **1.** the act of killing your own father. **2.** person who kills his or her father. –**pat′ri·cid′al,** adj.

pat·ri·ot·ic (pā′trē ot′ik), adj. **1.** loving your country. **2.** showing love and loyal support of your own country. –**pa′tri·ot′i·cal·ly,** adv.

pa·tron (pā′ trən), n. **1.** a regular customer; someone who buys regularly at a certain store or goes regularly to a certain restaurant, hotel, etc. **2.** person who gives approval and support to some person, art, cause, or undertaking: *A well-known patron of art, she has helped several young painters.*

patronize|prairie

pa·tron·ize (pā′trə nīz *or* pat′rə nīz), *v.* **1.** to be a regular customer of; give regular business to: *We patronize our neighborhood stores.* **2.** to act as a patron toward; support or protect: *patronize the ballet.*

pend·ing (pen′ding), **1.** *adj.* waiting to be decided or settled: *while the agreement was pending.* **2.** *prep.* while waiting for; until: *Pending your return, we'll get everything ready.*

pe·nin·su·la (pə nin′sə lə), *n.* piece of land almost surrounded by water, or extending far out into the water. Florida is a peninsula. *n., pl.* **pe·nin·su·las.** **–pe·nin′su·lar,** *adj.*

pen·sion (pen′shən), **1.** *n.* a regular payment by an employer or government to someone who is retired or disabled. **2.** *v.* to give a pension to: *The company pensioned several employees who were sixty-five years old.*

pe·num·bra (pi num′brə), *n.* the faint shadow beside the complete shadow cast by the sun, moon, or Earth during an eclipse. *n., pl.* **pe·num·bras, pe·num·brae** (pi num′brē).

per cap·i·ta (pər kap′ə tə), for each person: *a poor country with low per capita income.*

per·fi·dy (pėr′fə dē), *n.* being false to a trust; base treachery; a breaking faith.

per·jur·y (pėr′jər ē), *n.* act of swearing that something is true which you know to be false.

per·plexed (pər pleksd′) *adj.* troubled with doubt; puzzled; confused; bewildered: *The problem even perplexed the teacher.* **–per·plex′ed·ly,** *adv.* **–per·plex′ing·ly,** *adv.*

per·se·cute (pėr′sə kyüt), *v.* **1.** to treat badly; do harm to again and again; oppress: *Those bullies persecute the children by attacking them on their way home.* **2.** to treat badly because of your principles or beliefs: *Christians were persecuted in ancient Rome. v.* **per·se·cut·ed, per·se·cut·ing. –per′se·cu′tion,** *n.* **–per′se·cu′tor,** *n.*

per·sist·ent (pər sis′tənt), *adj.* **1.** refusing to stop or give up: *She was persistent in her demands for more freedom to choose her own clothing.* **2.** going on; continuing; lasting: *a persistent headache that lasted for days.* **–per·sist′ent·ly,** *adv.*

per·spi·ra·tion (pėr′spə rā′shən), *n.* **1.** sweat. **2.** process of sweating.

per·tain (pər tān′), *v.* **1.** to belong or be connected as a part or possession: *We own the house and the land pertaining to it.* **2.** to refer; be related: *My question pertains to yesterday's homework.*

phase (fāz), *n.* **1.** one of the changing stages of development of someone or something: *At present his voice is changing; this is a phase all boys go through.* **2.** the shape of the lighted part of the moon or a planet at a particular time.

pho·to·syn·the·sis (fō′tō sin′thə sis), *n.* process in which plant cells make carbohydrates from carbon dioxide and water in the presence of chlorophyll and light, and release oxygen as a by-product.

phys·i·cal (fiz′ə kəl), *adj.* **1.** of or for the body; bodily: *physical exercise.* **2.** of or about matter; material: *The tide is a physical force.*

phys·ics (fiz′iks), *n.* science that deals with matter and energy and the relationships between them. Physics includes the study of mechanics, heat, light, sound, electricity, magnetism, and atomic energy.

phys·i·ol·o·gy (fiz′ē ol′ə jē), *n.* **1.** branch of biology dealing with the normal functions of living things and their parts: *animal physiology, plant physiology.* **2.** all the functions and activities of a living thing or of any of its parts: *the physiology of the liver.* **–phys′i·o·log′i·cal,** *adj.* **–phys′i·ol′o·gist,** *n.*

phy·sique (fə zēk′), *n.* bodily structure or development; body.

pic·to·graph (pik′tə graf), *n.* **1.** picture used as a sign or symbol: *Chinese characters developed from pictographs.* **2.** chart or diagram showing facts or information by using pictures of different colors, sizes, or numbers. **–pic′to·graph′ic,** *adj.*

pis·til (pis′tl), *n.* the part of a flower that produces seeds, containing an ovary, a style, and a stigma.

plate (plāt), *n.* one of the large, slowly drifting, often continent-size sections of Earth's crust.

pli·ant (plī′ənt), *adj.* **1.** easily influenced; yielding: *a pliant nature.* **2.** changing easily to fit different conditions; adaptable. **–pli′ant·ly,** *adv.*

po·lit·i·cal par·ty (pə lit′ə kəl pär′tē), *n.* an organization concerned with getting and maintaining political power.

pol·li·na·tion (pol′ə nā′shən), *n.* the act of carrying pollen from anthers to pistils; bringing pollen to. Flowers are pollinated by bees, bats, birds, wind, etc. *v.* **pol·li·nat·ed, pol·li·nat·ing.**

pol·y·no·mi·al (pol′ē nō′mē əl), **1.** *n.* an algebraic expression containing two or more terms connected by plus signs or minus signs. **2.** *adj.* containing two or more algebraic terms.

post hoc (pōst′ häk), *adj.* taking place or done after an event.

prair·ie (prâr′ē), *n.* **1.** a large area of level or rolling land with grass but few or no trees, especially such an area making up much of central North America. **2. the Prairies,** *pl.* plain that covers southern and central Manitoba, Saskatchewan, and Alberta.

pre·cip·i·tate (pri sip′ə tit or pri sip′ə tāt), *n.* substance, usually crystalline, separated out from a solution as a solid.

pre·ci·sion (pri sizh′ən), *n.* condition of being exact; accuracy: *to speak with precision.*

pre·clude (pri klüd′), *v.* to shut out; make impossible; prevent: *The heavy thunderstorm precluded our going to the beach.* *v.* **pre·clud·ed, pre·clud·ing.**

pred·a·tor (pred′ə tər), *n.* animal or person that lives by killing and eating other animals.

pre·scrip·tion (pri skrip′shən), *n.* **1.** a written direction or order for preparing and using a medicine: *a prescription for cough medicine.* **2.** the medicine ordered.

pri·mate (prī′māt), *n.* one of a group of mammals that have very advanced brains and hands with thumbs that can grasp things. Primates are the most highly developed mammals. Apes, monkeys, lemurs, and human beings are primates. [**Primitive** comes from a Latin word meaning "first." So do **primacy, primary, primate,** and **prime.** In general, coming first suggests good things; when it happened long ago, however, it can suggest the absence of later advantages.]

prime (prīm), *adj.* first in rank; chief: *The town's prime need is a new school.*

pri·me·val (prī mē′vəl), *adj.* **1.** of or about the first age or ages, especially of the world: *In its primeval state Earth was without any forms of life.* **2.** ancient: *primeval forests untouched by the ax.* **–pri·me′val·ly,** *adv.*

prim·i·tive (prim′ə tiv), *adj.* **1.** of early times; of long ago: *Primitive people often lived in caves.* **2.** very simple; such as people had early in human history: *A primitive way of making fire is by rubbing two sticks together.*

prin·ci·pal·i·ty (prin′sə pal′ə tē), *n.* **1.** a small state or country ruled by a prince. **2.** the country from which a prince gets his title. *n., pl.* **prin·ci·pal·i·ties.**

prin·ci·ple (prin′sə pəl), *n.* **1.** a truth that is a foundation for other truths: *the principles of mathematics.* **2.** a fundamental belief: *religious principles.*

prism (priz′əm), *n.* **1.** a solid form with parallel ends that have the same size and shape, and with sides that have two pairs or parallel edges each. A six-sided pencil before it is sharpened has the form of one kind of prism. **2.** a transparent solid object, often made of glass, having the shape of a mathematical prism, usually with three-sided ends. Such objects can reflect or refract light, and some can separate white light into the colors of the spectrum by refraction.

priv·i·lege (priv′ə lij), *n.* a special right, advantage, or favor: *My sister has the privilege of driving the family car.* [**Privilege** comes from a Latin word meaning "a private law." Ancient Romans had a number of official laws for the benefit of one person or family.]

prob·a·bil·i·ty (prob′ə bil′ə tē), *n.* **1.** quality or fact of being likely or probable; good chance: *There is a probability of rain today.* **2.** a number that tells how likely it is that a certain event will occur. This number is the number of occurrences divided by the number of all possible occurrences. The probability that a coin will come up heads is $\frac{1}{2}$. *n., pl.* **prob·a·bil·i·ties.**

prog·no·sis (prog nō′sis), *n.* **1.** forecast of the probable course of a disease. **2.** estimate of what will probably happen. *n., pl.* **prog·no·ses** (prog nō′sēz).

prog·nos·ti·cate (prog nos′tə kāt), *v.* to tell what is going to happen; forecast. *v.* **prog·nos·ti·cat·ed, prog·nos·ti·cat·ing. –prog·nos′ti·ca′tion,** *n.* **–prog·nos′ti·ca·tor,** *n.*

pro·logue (prō′log), *n.* **1.** introduction to a novel, poem, or other literary work. **2.** speech or poem addressed to the audience by one of the actors at the beginning of a play.

pro·nun·ci·a·tion (prə nun′sē ā′shən), *n.* **1.** way of pronouncing. This book gives the pronunciation of each main word. **2.** act of making the sounds of words; speaking.

pro·pel (prə pel′), *v.* to drive forward; force ahead: *propel a boat by oars, a person propelled by ambition.* *v.* **pro·pelled, pro·pel·ling.**

pro·tein (prō′tēn), *n.* any of the many complex substances containing nitrogen that are necessary parts of the cells of animals and plants. Proteins are a necessary part of human and animal diets. Meat, milk, cheese, eggs, and beans contain protein. A protein is made of several or many amino acids.

pro·to·type (prō′tə tīp), *n.* the first or original type or model of anything that is designed or constructed.

pro·to·zo·an (prō′tə zō′ən), *n.* any of a great many living things that are like animals, but that have only one cell and are microscopic in size. Most protozoans live in water. They are neither animals nor plants, but another kind of life called protists. Amebas and paramecia are protozoans. *n., pl.* **pro·to·zo·ans, pro·to·zo·a** (prō′tə zō′ə).

psy·che (sī′kē), *n.* **1.** the human soul or spirit. **2.** the mind.

psy·chi·a·trist (sī kī′ə trist), *n.* doctor who treats mental and emotional disorders.

psy·chol·o·gy (sī kol′ə jē), *n.* **1.** science of the mind. Psychology tries to explain why people act, think, and feel as they do. **2.** the mental states and processes of a person or persons; mental nature and behavior: *The long illness had a bad effect on his psychology.*

psy·cho·so·mat·ic (sī′kō sə mat′ik), *adj.* of or about physical symptoms or diseases caused by psychological problems: *psychosomatic disorders.*

pul·sate (pul′sāt), *v.* **1.** to beat; throb: *The patient's heart was pulsating rapidly.* **2.** to vibrate; quiver. *v.* **pul·sat·ed, pul·sat·ing.**

GLOSSARY

punc·til·i·ous (pungk til′ē əs), *adj.* **1.** very careful and exact: *punctilious in details.* **2.** paying strict attention to details of conduct and ceremony. **–punc·til′i·ous·ly,** *adv.* **–punc·til′i·ous·ness,** *n.*

punc·tu·al (pungk′chü əl), *adj.* on time; prompt: *She is punctual to the minute.* **–punc·tu·al·i·ty** (pungk′chü al′ə tē), **punc′tu·al·ness,** *n.* **–punc′tu·al·ly,** *adv.*

punc·tu·a·tion (pungk′chü ā′shən), *n.* **1.** use of periods, commas, and other marks to help make the meaning of a sentence clear. Punctuation does for writing and printing what pauses and changes of voice do for speech. **2.** punctuation marks.

Qq

qua·drat·ic func·tion (kwä drat′ik fungk′shən), *n.* a function that can be described by an equation in the form of $f(x) = ax^2 + bx + x$, where $a \neq 0$. In quadratic functions, the greatest power of the variable is 2 and the resulting graph is a parabola.

quaint (kwānt), *adj.* strange or odd in an interesting, pleasing, or amusing way: *Many old photographs seem quaint to us today.* **–quaint′ly,** *adv.* **–quaint′ness,** *n.* [**Quaint** comes from a Latin word meaning "known" or "learned." In old times, **quaint** meant "skilled" or "cunning" or "stylish." Styles change, and things that looked smart once look strange now.]

Rr

ra·di·us (rā′dē əs), *n.* **1.** a line segment going straight from the center to the outside of a circle or a sphere. Any spoke in a wheel is a radius. **2.** the length of such a line segment: *The radius of the circle is 6 centimeters. n., pl.* **ra·di·i** or **ra·di·us·es.**

range (rānj), *n.* (in mathematics) **a.** the set of all the values a given function may take on. **b.** a domain.

rate of change, *n.* the speed or pace at which a variable changes over time.

ra·ti·o (rā′shē ō), *n.* **1.** relation between two quantities expressed as a quotient. "They have sheep and cows in the ratio of 10 to 3" means that they have ten sheep for every three cows. **2.** quotient expressing this relation. The ratio between two quantities is the number of times one contains the other. The ratio of 10 to 3 is written as 10:3, 10/3, 10 ÷ 3, or $\frac{10}{3}$. The ratios of 3 to 5 and 6 to 10 are the same. *n., pl.* **ra·ti·os.** [**Ratio** comes from a Latin word meaning "calculation" or "arithmetic." **Reason** and **rational** come from the same word. Arithmetic is a purely reasonable activity that achieves rational results.]

ra·tion (rash′ən *or* rā′shən), *n.* **1.** a fixed allowance of food; the daily allowance of food for a person or animal.

2. portion of anything dealt out; share; allotment: *After the flood, volunteers gave out food rations to homeless people.*

ray (rā), *n.* a beam of light: *rays of the sun.* **2.** the part of a line on one side of any particular point on the line; half-line. [**Ray** comes from a Latin word meaning "spoke of a wheel."]

re·al·ism (rē′ə liz′əm), *n.* **1.** thought and action based on realities: *Her realism cause her to dislike fanciful schemes.* **2.** (in art and literature) the picturing of life as it actually is.

re·al·is·tic (rē′ə lis′tik), *adj.* **1.** like the real thing; lifelike: *The speaker gave a very realistic picture of life a hundred years ago.* **2.** seeing things as they are; practical: *She wanted to buy a car, but decided to be realistic and save her money for college.* **–re′al·is′ti·cal·ly,** *adv.*

re·cip·ro·cal (ri sip′rə kəl), **1.** *adj.* in return: *Although she gave me a present, she expected no reciprocal gift from me.* **2.** *adj.* existing on both sides; mutual: *reciprocal liking, reciprocal distrust.* **3.** *n.* number so related to another that when multiplied together they give 1: *3 is the reciprocal of $\frac{1}{3}$. and $\frac{1}{3}$ is the reciprocal of 3.*

rec·luse (rek′lüs *or* ri klüs), *n.* someone who lives alone, away from society.

re·cog·ni·zance (ri kog′nə zəns), *n.* (in law) **a.** an agreement made in court by which someone promises to do something, such as to come to court again. **b.** sum of money to be given up if the thing is not done.

re·coil (ri koil′), *v.* **1.** to pull yourself back; shrink back: *Most people would recoil at seeing a snake.* **2.** to spring back: *The gun recoiled after I fired it.* [**Recoil** comes from two Latin words meaning "back" and "rump," used to suggest falling down into sitting position. In the past, **recoil** meant a much larger backward movement than it does now.]

rec·on·cile (rek′ən sīl), *v.* **1.** to make friends again: *The children had quarreled but were soon reconciled.* **2.** to settle a quarrel or difference: *The teacher reconciled the dispute between the two pupils.* **3.** to make agree; bring into harmony: *It is impossible to reconcile the story with the facts. v.* **rec·on·ciled, rec·on·cil·ing. –rec′on·cile′ment,** *n.* **–rec′on·cil′er,** *n.*

re·fute (ri fyüt′), *v.* to show that a claim, opinion, or argument is false or incorrect; prove wrong; disprove: *He refuted the rumors with facts. v.* **re·fut·ed, re·fut·ing. –ref·u·ta·tion** (ref′yə tā′shən), *n.* **–re·fut′er,** *n.*

re·gres·sion (ri gresh′ən), *n.* a relationship between several correlated variables which shows the average value of a variable given that one or more of the independent variables have specified values.

rep·e·ti·tious (rep′ə tish′əs), *adj.* full of repetitions; repeating in a tiresome way: *repetitious excuses.* **–rep′e·ti′tious·ly,** *adv.* **–rep′e·ti′tious·ness,** *n.*

rep·re·sent·a·tive (rep′ri zen′ tə tiv), *n.* **1.** person appointed or elected to act or speak for others: *She is the club's representative at the convention.* **2.** member of the House of Representatives.

re·pul·sive (ri pul′siv), *adj.* **1.** causing strong dislike or aversion: *the repulsive smell of a skunk.* **2.** tending to drive back or repel. **–re·pul′sive·ly,** *adv.* **–re·pul′sive·ness,** *n.*

re·sent (ri zent′), *v.* to feel injured and angry at; feel indignation at: *I resented being called lazy.*

re·sid·u·al (ri zij′ü əl), *n.* difference between a value measured and the true value. **–re·sid′u·al·ly,** *adv.*

re·sist·ance (ri zis′təns), *n.* **1.** act of resisting: *The bank clerk made no resistance to the robbers.* **2.** power to resist: *Some people have very little resistance to colds.*

res·o·lute (rez′ə lüt), *adj.* determined; firm: *be resolute against all opposition. She was resolute in her attempt to climb to the top of the mountain.* **–res′o·lute′ly,** *adv.* **–res′o·lute′ness,** *n.*

res·o·nate (rez′n āt), *v.* to produce full, vibrant sound; resound. *v.* **res·o·nat·ed, res·o·nat·ing.**

res·ti·tu·tion (res′tə tü′shən), *n.* **1.** act of giving back what has been lost or taken away. **2.** act of making good any loss, damage, or injury: *It is only fair that those who do the damage should make restitution.*

re·tort (ri tôrt′), *v.* reply quickly or sharply: *"It's none of your business," I retorted.*

re·vi·sion (ri vizh′ən), *n.* **1.** act of working or revising. **2.** a revised form: *a revision of a book.*

rid·i·cule (rid′ə kyül), **1.** *v.* to laugh at; make fun of: *People once ridiculed the idea of an airplane.* **2.** *n.* laughter in mockery; words or actions that make fun of somebody or something: *I was very hurt by the ridicule of my classmates. v.* **rid·i·culed, rid·i·cul·ing. –rid′icul·er,** *n.*

rise (rīz), *n.* **1.** (in mathematics) the vertical height of a step, slope, arch, etc. **2.** an upward slope: *a rise in a road. The rise of that hill is gradual.*

run (run), *n.* (in mathematics) the horizontal length of a line, slope, arch, etc.

Ss

sa·la·mi (sə lä′mē), *n.* kind of thick sausage, often flavored with garlic. It is usually sliced and eaten cold. *n., pl.* **sa·la·mis.** [**Salami** comes from a Latin word meaning "salt." Salami contains much salt, which helps to preserve it.]

sa·line (sā′lēn), **1.** *adj.* of or like salt; salty. **2.** *n.* solution with a high concentration of salt, used in medical examinations and treatment.

sa·lin·i·ty (sə lin′ə tē), *n.* saline condition or quality; saltiness.

salt·wa·ter (sòlt′wò′tər), *adj.* **1.** made up of salt and water: *a saltwater solution.* **2.** living in the sea or in water like seawater: *saltwater fish.*

sar·casm (sär′kaz′əm), *n.* **1.** a sneering or cutting remark, often ironical. **2.** act of making fun of someone to hurt his or her feelings; harsh or bitter irony: *"How unselfish you are!" said the girl in sarcasm as her sister took the biggest piece of cake.* [**Sarcasm** comes from a Greek word meaning "to strip off flesh." Today we speak of cutting remarks that can wound feelings. Words used as weapons can cause serious pain.]

scatter plot, *n.* a graph which uses scattered points to show the relationship between multiple sets of data.

scav·en·ger (skav′ən jər), *n.* **1.** living thing that feeds on decaying matter. Vultures and jackals are scavengers. **2.** person who searches through discarded objects for something of value. [**Scavenger** comes from a Flemish word meaning "to inspect." In old times, Flemish tax inspectors were also required to clean the streets. They liked to be called inspectors, but people thought of them as garbage collectors.]

scene (sēn), *n.* **1.** part of an act of a play: *The queen comes to the castle in Act 1, Scene 2.* **2.** a particular incident of a play: *The scene in which the detective reveals the name of the murderer is the highlight of the play.*

se·clud·ed (si klü′did), *adj.* shut off from others; undisturbed: *He wrote that famous novel at a secluded cottage in the woods.* **–se·clud′ed·ly,** *adv.* **–se·clud′ed·ness,** *n.*

se·clus·ion (si klü′zhən), *n.* **1.** condition of being secluded; retirement: *She lives in seclusion apart from her friends.* **2.** a secluded place.

sec·ond·ar·y (sek′ən der′ē), *adj.* **1.** next after the first in order, place, time, or importance: *A secondary industry uses products of other industries as its raw materials.* **2.** not main or chief; having less importance: *Reading fast is secondary to reading well.* **–sec′ond·ar′i·ly,** *adv.* **–sec′ond·ar′i·ness,** *n.*

sect (sekt), *n.* group of people having the same principles, beliefs, or opinions: *a religious sect.*

sem·i·co·lon (sem′i kō′lən), *n.* mark of punctuation (;) that shows a separation not so complete as that shown by a period but more so than that shown by a comma. EXAMPLE: We arrived later than we had intended; consequently there was little time left for swimming before the volleyball game.

sem·i·con·duc·tor (sem′i kən duk′tər), *n.* a mineral substance, such as silicon, that conducts electricity better than an insulator but not so well as a metal. Semiconductors can convert alternating current into direct current and amplify weak electric signals. Transistors are made primarily of semiconductors.

GLOSSARY

sem·i·fi·nal (sem′i fī′nl *for adj.*; sem′i fī′nl *for noun*), **1.** *adj.* of or about the two games, matches, or rounds that come before the final one in a tournament. **2.** *n.* often, **semifinals,** *pl.* one of these two games.

sem·i·month·ly (sem′i munth′lē), **1.** *adj.* occurring or appearing twice a month. **2.** *n.* magazine or newspaper published twice a month. *n., pl.* **sem·i·month·lies.**

sem·i·pro·fes·sion·al (sem′i prə fesh′ə nəl), **1.** *n.* a part-time professional athlete. **2.** *adj.* about or for such athletes. **–sem′i·pro·fes′sion·al·ly,** *adv.*

sen·sa·tion (sen sā′shən), *n.* **1.** feeling: *Ice gives a sensation of coldness.* **2.** action of the senses; power to see, hear, feel, taste, smell, etc.: *An unconscious person is without sensation.*

sen·sor·y (sen′sər ē), *adj.* of or about sensation of the senses. The eyes and ears are sensory organs.

sen·su·ous (sen′shü əs), *adj.* **1.** of or derived from the senses; having an effect on the senses; perceived by the senses: *the sensuous thrill of a warm bath, a sensuous love of color.* **2.** enjoying the pleasures of the senses. **–sen′su·ous·ly,** *adv.* **–sen′su·ous·ness,** *n.*

sen·tient (sen′shənt), *adj.* able to feel; having feeling: *sentient beings.* **–sen′tient·ly,** *adv.*

se·ques·ter (si kwes′tər), *v.* to remove or withdraw from public use or from public view: *The author sequestered herself in a seaside cottage while she worked on her new book.*

se·rene (sə rēn′), *adj.* **1.** peaceful; calm: *a serene smile.* **2.** not cloudy; clear; bright: *a serene sky.* **–se·rene′ly,** *adv.* **–se·rene′ness,** *n.*

sin·is·ter (sin′ə stər), *adj.* **1.** bad; evil; dishonest: *a sinister plan.* **2.** showing ill will; threatening: *a sinister rumor, a sinister look.* **–sin′is·ter·ly,** *adv.* **–sin′is·ter·ness,** *n.* [**Sinister** comes from a Latin word meaning "on the left side." The ancient Romans tried to predict the future by omens—events that people thought were signs of what would happen. Their omens included birds in flight or a bolt of lightning. Omens on the left side were thought to mean bad luck, so the Latin word also meant "unlucky." In English the meaning is even more negative.]

slope (slōp), *n.* **1.** amount of slant. **2.** the tangent of the angle formed by the intersection of a straight line with the x-axis.

so·lar·i·um (sə lâr′ē əm), *n.* room, porch, etc., where people can lie or sit in the sun. *n., pl.* **so·lar·i·ums, so·lar·i·a** (səl âr′ē ə).

sole (sōl), *adj.* one and only; single: *He was the sole heir to the fortune when his aunt died.*

so·lil·o·quy (sə lil′ə kwē), *n.* **1.** speech made by an actor to himself or herself. It reveals the actor's thoughts and feelings to the audience, but not to the other characters in the play. **2.** act of talking to yourself. *n., pl.* **so·lil·o·quies.**

sol·i·tar·y (sol′ə ter′ē), *adj.* **1.** without companions; away from people; lonely. **2.** alone; single; only: *A solitary rider was seen in the distance.* **–sol′i·tar′i·ly,** *adv.* **–sol′i·tar′i·ness,** *n.*

sol·i·tude (sol′ə tüd), *n.* **1.** condition of being alone: *He likes company and hates solitude.* **2.** loneliness.

so·lo (sō′lō), *adj.* without a partner, teacher, etc.; alone: *The flying student made her first solo flight.*

so·lo·ist (sō′lō ist), *n.* person who sings or plays a solo or solos.

sol·stice (sol′stis), *n.* either of the two times in the year when the sun appears to be farthest north or south in the sky. In the Northern Hemisphere, June 21 or 22, the **summer solstice,** is the longest day of the year and December 21 or 22, the **winter solstice,** is the shortest.

son·ic (son′ik), *adj.* **1.** of or about sound waves. **2.** of or about the rate at which sound travels through air. At sea level the rate is 1087 feet (331 meters) per second. **–son′i·cal·ly,** *adv.*

so·nor·ous (sə nôr′əs), *adj.* **1.** giving out or having a deep loud sound: *a big, sonorous church bell.* **2.** having an impressive sound; high-sounding: *sonorous phases, a sonorous style.* **–so·no′rous·ly,** *adv.*

speed·om·e·ter (spē dom′ə tər), *n.* **1.** device to show the speed of a motor vehicle. **2.** odometer.

spir·it (spir′it), *n.* **1.** the part of a human being that is not bodily; soul: *Some religions teach that at death the spirit leaves the body.* **2.** a person's moral, religious, or emotional nature: *a proud spirit.* **3.** Often, **spirits,** *pl.* state of mind; mood; temper: *She is in good spirits.* **4.** courage; vigor; liveliness: *A show horse must have spirit.* **5.** enthusiasm and loyalty: *team spirit.*

sprawl (sprôl), *v.* **1.** to lie or sit with the arms and legs spread out, especially in an awkward manner: *The children were sprawled in front of the TV.* **2.** to spread out in an irregular or awkward manner: *His large handwriting sprawled across the page.*

square root, *n.* number that produces a given number when multiplied by itself: *The square root of 16 is 4.*

stage direction, *n.* a direction in a written or printed play to indicate the appropriate action, arrangement of the stage, etc.

stag·ing (stā′jing), *n.* act or process of putting a play on the stage.

sta·men (stā′mən), *n.* the part of the flower that contains the pollen. A stamen has a slender stem that supports the anther.

standard deviation, *n.* a measure of how tightly a set of numbers are clustered around the mean, or average, of the set.

starch (stärch), *n.* a white, tasteless food substance. Potatoes, wheat, rice, and corn contain much starch.

sta·tion (stā′shən), *n.* building or place used for a definite purpose: *a police station.*

sta·tis·tic (stə tis′tik), *n.* any value, item, etc., used in the science of collecting and using numerical facts about people, the weather, business conditions, etc.

stat·ure (stach′ər), *n.* **1.** height: *a young woman of average stature.* **2.** physical, mental, or moral growth; accomplishment: *Thomas Jefferson was a man of great stature among his countrymen.*

sta·tus (stā′təs *or* stat′əs), *n.* **1.** social or professional standing; position; rank: *to lose status, to seek status. What is her status in the government?* **2.** state; condition: *Diplomats are interested in the status of world affairs.*

stat·ute (stach′üt), *n.* law enacted by a legislative group: *The statutes for the United States are made by Congress.*

stealth·y (stel′thē), *adj.* done in a secret manner; secret; sly: *The cat crept in a stealthy way toward the bird. adj.* **stealth·i·er, stealth·i·est.** –**stealth′i·ly,** –**stealth′i·ness,** *n.*

ster·e·o·type (ster′ē ə tīp′ *or* stir′ē ə tīp′), **1.** *n.* an oversimplified conventional notion or idea about a person, group, thought, etc., held in common by members of a group, and which allows for no individual judgments. Long John Silver, in Stevenson's *Treasure Island,* is the stereotype of a pirate. **2.** *v.* to give a fixed or settled form to. *v.* **ster·e·o·typed, ster·e·o·typ·ing.** –**ster′e·o·typ′er,** *n.* –**ster·e·o·typ·ic** (ster′ē ə tip′ik *or* stir′ē ə tip′ik), **ster′e·o·typ′i·cal,** *adj.* –**ster′e·o·typ′i·cal·ly,** *adv.*

stim·u·late (stim′yə lāt), *v.* **1.** to make more active; encourage; rouse to action: *The new factory helped to stimulate the growth of the town.* **2.** to act as a stimulant or a stimulus. *v.* **stim·u·lat·ed, stim·u·lat·ing.** –**stim′u·la′tion,** *n.* –**stim′u·lat′or** *or* **stim′u·la′ter,** *n.*

stress (stres), **1.** *n.* loudness in the pronunciation of syllables, words in a sentence, etc.; accent: *In "zero," the stress is on the first syllable.* **2.** *v.* to pronounce with stress: *"Accept" is stressed on the second syllable. n., pl.* **stress·es.**

stur·dy (stėr′dē), *adj.* **1.** strong; stout: *a sturdy chair.* **2.** not yielding; firm: *The enemy put up a sturdy defense. adj.* **stur·di·er, stur·di·est.** –**stur′di·ly,** *adv.* –**stud′di·ness,** *n.*

sub·se·quent·ly (sub′sə kwənt lē), *adv.* coming after; later: *She subsequently proved that she was right.*

sub·si·dize (sub′sə dīz), *v.* to aid or assist with a grant of money: *The government subsidizes airlines that carry mail. v.* **sub·si·dized, sub·si·diz·ing.** –**sub′si·di·za′tion,** *n.* –**sub′si·diz′er,** *n.*

sub·ur·ban (sə bėr′bən), *adj.* **1.** of or in a suburb: *We have excellent suburban train service.* **2.** like a suburb or its inhabitants.

sub·ur·ban·ite (sə bėr′bə nīt), *n.* person who lives in a suburb.

su·per·fi·cial (sü′pər fish′əl), *adj.* **1.** of, on, or at the surface: *superficial measurement. His burns were superficial and soon healed.* **2.** concerned with or understanding only what is on the surface; not thorough; shallow: *superficial knowledge.* **su′per·fi′ci·al·ly,** *adv.* –**su′per·fi′cial·ness,** *n.*

sup·pli·ca·tion (sup′lə kā′shən), *n.* **1.** a humble and earnest request or prayer: *Supplications to God arose from many people in the besieged town.* **2.** act of supplicating or asking.

surface area, *n.* the total area of a two-dimensional or three-dimensional object.

sus·pense·ful (sə spens′fəl), *adj.* characterized by or full of suspense.

sym·bi·ot·ic (sim′bē ot′ik), *adj.* of or living in symbiosis, or the condition in which two unlike living things live together for the benefit of each. –**sym′bi·ot′i·cal·ly,** *adv.*

sym·bol (sim′bəl), *n.* something that stands for or represents something else.

sym·met·ric (si met′rik), *adj.* symmetrical: *symmetric patterns.*

symp·tom (simp′təm), *n.* **1.** a sign or indication: *Shaking knees and paleness are symptoms of fear or shock.* **2.** a noticeable change in the normal working of the body that indicates or accompanies disease, sickness, etc.: *The doctor made her diagnosis after studying the patient's symptoms.*

syn·chro·nize (sing′krə nīz), *v.* **1.** to make agree in time: *synchronize all the clocks in a building.* **2.** to occur at the same time, agree in time. *v.* **syn·chro·nized, syn·chro·niz·ing.** –**syn′chro·ni·za′tion,** *n.*

syn·tax (sin′taks), *n.* **1.** way in which the words and phrases of a sentence are arranged to show how they relate to each other. **2.** part of grammar dealing with this.

syn·thet·ic (sin thet′ik), *adj.* **1.** made artificially by chemical synthesis. Nylon is a synthetic fiber. **2.** not real or genuine; artificial: *synthetic laughter.* –**syn·thet′i·cal·ly,** *adv.*

Tt

tact (takt), *n.* ability to say and do the right things; skill in dealing with people or handling difficult situations: *Mother's tact kept her from talking about things likely to be unpleasant to her guests.*

tactful|typographical

tact·ful (takt′fəl), *adj.* **1.** having tact: *a tactful person.* **2.** showing tact: *a tactful reply.* –**tact′ful·ly**, *adv.* –**tact′ful·ness**, *n.*

tac·tile (tak′təl), *adj.* **1.** of or about touch. **2.** having the sense of touch.

tan·gent (tan′jənt), *adj.* in contact; touching.

tel·e·cast (tel′ə kast′), **1.** *v.* to broadcast by television. **2.** *n.* a TV broadcast. *v.* **tel·e·cast** or **tel·e·cast·ed**, **tel·e·cast·ing.** –**tel′e·cast′er.**

tel·e·com·mute (tel′ə kə myüt′), *v.* to work for a business while at home, by using telecommunication devices, especially a computer with a modem, to communicate with your office: *She telecommutes on Thursdays but is in the office the rest of the week. v.* **tel·e·com·mut·ed**, **tel·e·com·mut·ing.** –**tel′e·com·mut′er**, *n.*

tel·e·gen·ic (tel′ə jen′ik), *adj.* suitable for telecasting.

te·lep·a·thy (tə lep′ə thē), *n.* communication of one mind with another without using speech, hearing, sight, or any other sense used normally to communicate.

tel·e·pho·to (tel′ə fō′tō), *adj.* of or relating to a photographic lens used to produce an enlarged image of a distant object.

tel·e·scope (tel′ə skōp), *n.* device for making distant objects appear nearer and larger. Objects in space are studied by means of telescopes.

te·na·cious (ti nā′shəs), *adj.* **1.** stubborn; persistent: *a tenacious salesman.* **2.** holding fast: *the tenacious jaws of a bulldog.* –**te·na′cious·ly**, *adv.* –**te·na′cious·ness**, *n.*

ten·ant (ten′ənt), *n.* **1.** person paying rent for the use of land, a building, or space in a building belonging to another person: *That building has apartments for one hundred tenants.* **2.** person or thing that occupies: *Wild animals were the only tenants of the forest.* –**ten′ant·less**, *adj.*

ten·den·tious (ten den′shəs), *adj.* having a tendency to show only one side; one-sided: *a tendentious statement.* **ten·den′tious·ly**, *adv.* –**ten·den′tious·ness**, *n.*

ter·ror·ism (ter′ə riz′əm), *n.* use of terror or violence.

ther·mal (thėr′məl), **1.** *adj.* of or about heat. **2.** *n.* a rising current of warm air. –**ther′mal·ly**, *adv.*

ther·mos (thėr′məs), *n.* container made with a vacuum between its inner and outer walls so that its contents remain hot or cold for a long time.

to·pog·ra·phy (tə pog′rə fē), *n.* **1.** the surface features of a place or region, such as hills, valleys, streams, lakes, bridges, tunnels, roads, etc. **2.** act or process of preparing an accurate and detailed description or drawing of a region's or place's surface features.

tor·tu·ous (tôr′chü əs), *adj.* **1.** full of twists, turns, or bends; twisting; winding; crooked: *We found the river's course very tortuous.* **2.** mentally or morally crooked; not straightforward: *tortuous reasoning.* –**tor′tu·ous·ly**, *adv.* –**tor′tu·ous·ness**, *n.*

tract (trakt), *n.* area of land, buildings, etc.; district: *a tract of desert land.*

trans·la·tion (tran slā′shən *or* tranz lā′shən), *n.* **1.** result of translating; version: *A Spanish translation of a book.* **2.** act or process of changing into another language: *the translation of the Bible from Hebrew into Latin.*

tran·spire (tran spīr′), *v.* to take place; happen: *I heard later what transpired at the meeting.*

trans·pose (tran spōz′), *v.* **1.** to change the usual order of letters, words, or numbers: *I transposed the numbers and mistakenly wrote 19 for 91.* **2.** to transfer a term to the other side of an algebraic equation, changing plus to minus or minus to plus. *v.* **trans·posed, trans·pos·ing.** –**trans·pos′a·ble**, *adj.* –**trans·pos′er**, *n.*

trea·son (trē′zn), *n.* betrayal of your country or ruler. Helping the enemies of your country is treason. [**Treason** comes from a Latin word meaning "to hand over." **Traitor** comes from the same Latin word, and so does **tradition**. When a traitor hands over plans to the enemy, that's treason. When parents or teachers hand over customs to young people, that's tradition.]

trib·u·tar·y (trib′yə ter′ē), *n.* stream that flows into a larger one: *The Ohio River is a tributary of the Mississippi River. n., pl.* **trib·u·tar·ies.**

tri·umph (trī′umf), **1.** *n.* victory; success: *final triumph over the enemy. The exploration of outer space is a great triumph of modern science.* **2.** *v.* to gain victory; win success: *Our team triumphed over theirs.* **3.** *n.* joy because of victory or success: *We welcomed the team home with cheers of triumph.*

tro·pism (trō′piz′əm), *n.* tendency of a living thing to turn or move in response to a stimulus, such as light or gravity.

type·cast (tīp′kast′), *v.* **1.** cast (an actor) in a role that seems to suit the actor's appearances and personality. **2.** cast repeatedly in the same role.

typ·i·cal (tip′ə kəl), *adj.* **1.** showing the features of a group or kind: *The typical Thanksgiving dinner consists of turkey, cranberry sauce, several vegetables, and mince or pumpkin pie.* **2.** of or descriptive of a type; characteristic: *the hospitality typical of frontier people.*

typ·ist (tī′pist), *n.* person who types on a typewriter or a computer keyboard.

ty·po·graph·i·cal (tī′pə graf′ə kəl), *adj.* of or about printing or typing: *"Catt" and "cOw" contain typographical errors.* –**ty′po·graph′i·cal·ly**, *adv.*

ty·pog·ra·phy (tī pog′rə fē), *n.* **1.** art or process of printing with type; work of setting and arranging type and printing from it. **2.** arrangement, appearance, or style of printed matter.

Uu

um·brage (um′brij), *n.* the foliage of trees, etc., providing shade.

u·ni·son (yü′nə sən), *n.* **1.** agreement: *The marchers' feet moved in unison. We spoke in unison.* **2.** agreement in pitch of two or more tones, voices, etc.; a sounding together at the same pitch. [**Unison** comes from Latin words meaning "one" and "sound." People who say the same thing in the same way must really agree.]

un·ten·a·ble (un′ten′ə bəl), *adj.* not able to be defended.

ur·bane (ėr′bān′), *adj.* courteous, refined, or elegant: *urbane manners.* **–ur′bane′ly,** *adv.*

ur·ban·i·za·tion (ėr′bə nə zā′shən), *n.* the act, process, or state of being urbanized: *The urbanization of the countryside greatly changed the landscape.*

u·ten·sil (yü ten′səl), *n.* **1.** container or implement used for practical purposes. Pots and pans are kitchen utensils. **2.** device or tool used for some special purpose. Pens and pencils are writing utensils.

Vv

va·can·cy (vā′kən sē), *n.* **1.** a room, space, or apartment for rent; empty space: *a vacancy in the motel, a vacancy in the parking lot.* **2.** condition of being vacant; emptiness. *n., pl.* **va·can·cies** for 1.

va·cate (vā′kāt), *v.* to go away from and leave empty or unoccupied; make vacant: *They will vacate the house on May 1. v.* **va·cat·ed, va·cat·ing.**

va·ca·tion (vā kā′shən), *n.* freedom from school, business, or other duties: *There is a vacation from school every summer.*

va·cu·i·ty (va kyü′ə tē), *n.* **1.** an empty space; vacuum. **2.** emptiness of mind; lack of ideas or intelligence.

vac·u·ous (vak′yü əs), *adj.* **1.** showing no intelligence; stupid. **2.** empty. **–vac′u·ous·ly,** *adv.* **–vac′u·ous·ness,** *n.*

vac·u·um (vak′yü əm *or* vak′yüm), *n.* **1.** a space that has almost no air or other matter in it. Outer space is a vacuum of this sort. **2.** an emptiness; void: *Their child's death left a vacuum in their lives.*

var·i·able (vâr′ē bəl), **1.** *n.* thing or quality that varies. **2.** *n.* (in mathematics) **a.** quantity that can assume any of a given set of values. **b.** symbol representing this quantity. **–var′i·a·ble·ness,** *n.* **–var′i·a·bly,** *adv.*

ven·tril·o·quist (ven tril′ə kwist), *n.* person skilled in ventriloquism, or the art or practice of speaking with the lips shut so the voice may seem to come from some source other than the speaker.

ver·tex (vėr′teks), *n.* **1.** the highest point; top. **2.** (in geometry) **a.** point opposite the base of a triangle, pyramid, etc. **b.** the point where the two sides of an angle meet. *n., pl.* **ver·tex·es, ver·ti·ces** (vėr′tə sēz).

vig·or·ous (vig′ər əs), *adj.* full of vigor; strong and active; energetic; forceful: *a vigorous and lively man. Doctors wage a vigorous war against disease.* **–vig′or·ous·ly,** *adv.* **–vig′or·ous·ness,** *n.*

vir·tue (vėr′chü), *n.* **1.** moral excellence; goodness: *a person of the highest virtue.* **2.** a good quality: *She praised the virtues of her small car.*

vi·rus (vī′rəs), *n.* a very small germ formed of protein and nucleic acid. Viruses are smaller than any known bacteria and cannot be seen through most microscopes. They can reproduce only inside the cells of living things. Viruses cause rabies, polio, chicken pox, the common cold, and many other diseases. *n., pl.* **vi·rus·es.** [**Virus** comes from a Latin word meaning "poison." For a long time, people had no idea what viruses were, so they thought that many diseases were caused by some sort of poison. After viruses were discovered, the name was too familiar to change.]

vi·ta·min (vī′tə mən), **1.** *n.* any of certain special substances necessary in small amounts for the normal growth and proper nourishment of the body, found especially in milk, butter, raw fruits and vegetables, cod-liver oil, and the outside part of wheat and other grains. Lack of essential vitamins causes such diseases as rickets and scurvy, as well as generally poor health. **2.** *adj.* of or containing vitamins: *a vitamin tablet, a vitamin deficiency.*

Zz

zo·di·ac (zō′dē ak), *n.* **1.** the section of the sky through which the location of sunrise moves north and south each year. It is divided into 12 equal parts called signs, named for 12 constellations found in them. **2.** diagram representing the zodiac, used in astrology. **–zo·di·a·cal** (zō dī′ə kəl), *adj.* [**Zodiac** comes from a Greek word meaning "animal." Because so many signs of the zodiac are constellations named for animals, ancient Greeks called this part of the sky the circle of the animals.]

zon·ing (zō′ning), *n.* building restrictions in an area of a city or town.

zo·ol·o·gy (zō ol′ə jē), *n.* the science of animals; the study of animals and animal life. Zoology is a branch of biology. **–zo·ol′o·gist,** *n.*

Word Part List

These are the word parts—the roots, prefixes, and suffixes—taught in this book. They are listed in alphabetical order, going from left to right. Each entry gives you the following information:

- identification of the word part as root, prefix, or suffix
- other ways to spell the word part
- language origin of the word part, usually Latin or Greek
- meaning of the word part
- anchor word that contains the word part to help you remember its meaning

prefix **anti**
origin Greek
meaning against
anchor word antibacterial

root **aqu**
origin Latin
meaning water
anchor word aquarium

prefix **ab**
origin Latin
meaning off, away, *or* down
anchor word absent

root **aer**
origin Greek
meaning air
anchor word aerobics

root **agr**
origin Latin
meaning field
anchor word agriculture

root **cata**
origin Greek
meaning down
anchor word cataract

root **centr**
origin Latin
meaning center
anchor word center

root **bio**
origin Greek
meaning life
anchor word biology

root **cand**
origin Latin
meaning shine
anchor word candle

root **cap**
origin Latin
meaning head
anchor word cap

root **chrom**
origin Greek
meaning color
anchor word chrome

root **chron**
origin Greek
meaning time
anchor word synchronize

suffix **cide**
origin Latin
meaning kill
anchor word insecticide

root **cipher**
origin Latin
meaning code
anchor word decipher

root **cred**
origin Latin
meaning believe
anchor word incredible

prefix **fore**
origin Old English
meaning before *or* beforehand
anchor word forecast

root **cis**
origin Latin
meaning cut
anchor word scissors

root **dem**
origin Greek
meaning people
anchor word democracy

root **frat**
origin Latin
meaning brother
anchor word fraternity

root **clud**
other spellings clus
origin Latin
meaning close *or* shut
anchor word secluded

root **doc**
origin Latin
meaning teach
anchor word documentary

root **gno**
origin Greek
meaning to know
anchor word diagnose

root **cogn**
origin Latin
meaning to know
anchor word recognize

root **fid**
origin Latin
meaning trust
anchor word confidence

root **graph**
other spellings gram
origin Greek
meaning write
anchor word autograph

root **corp**
origin Latin
meaning body
anchor word corpse

root **flu**
origin Latin
meaning flow
anchor word fluid

root **hydr**
origin Greek
meaning water *or* fluid
anchor word hydrant

suffix **ism**
origin Greek
meaning condition *or* belief
anchor word egotism

root **leg**
origin Latin
meaning law
anchor word legal

root **lu**
origin Latin
meaning wash
anchor word dilute

root **ject**
origin Latin
meaning throw
anchor word eject

root **lingu**
origin Latin
meaning language
anchor word linguistics

root **mat**
origin Latin
meaning mother
anchor word maternity

root **jur**
other spellings jud, jus
origin Latin
meaning law
anchor word jury

root **lit**
origin Latin
meaning writing *or* letter
anchor word literature

root **meter**
origin Greek
meaning measure
anchor word millimeter

root **junct**
origin Latin
meaning join
anchor word conjunction

root **log**
origin Greek
meaning word
anchor word dialogue

root **nav**
origin Latin
meaning ship
anchor word navy

root **lau**
other spellings lav
origin Latin
meaning wash
anchor word laundry

root **loq**
other spellings loc
origin Latin
meaning speak
anchor word eloquent

root **pat**
origin Latin
meaning father
anchor word paternal

root **path**

origin Greek

meaning feeling, emotion, suffer, disease

anchor word empathy

root **prim**

other spellings princ

origin Latin

meaning first

anchor word primary

prefix **semi**

origin Latin

meaning half

anchor word semicircle

root **pel**

other spellings puls

origin Latin

meaning drive *or* push

anchor word expel

root **psych**

origin Greek

meaning mind *or* spirit

anchor word psychic

root **sent**

other spellings sens

origin Latin

meaning to feel

anchor word sentiment

root **pend**

other spellings pens

origin Latin

meaning hang, weigh, *or* pay

anchor word pendulum

root **punct**

origin Latin

meaning point *or* dot

anchor word puncture

root **sequ**

other spellings sec

origin Latin

meaning follow

anchor word sequence

root **phys**

origin Greek

meaning nature *or* natural

anchor word physician

root **rid**

other spellings ris

origin Latin

meaning laugh

anchor word ridiculous

root **sol**

origin Latin

meaning alone

anchor word solo

root **plex**

other spellings pli, ply

origin Latin

meaning fold *or* twine

anchor word duplex

root **sal**

origin Latin

meaning salt

anchor word salt

root **sol**

origin Latin

meaning sun

anchor word solar

root **son**
origin Latin
meaning sound
anchor word consonant

root **tang**
other spellings tact
origin Latin
meaning touch
anchor word tangible

root **umbr**
origin Latin
meaning shadow *or* shade
anchor word umbrella

root **spir**
origin Latin
meaning breathe
anchor word respiration

prefix **tele**
origin Greek
meaning far *or* distant
anchor word television

root **urb**
origin Latin
meaning city
anchor word urban

root **sta**
other spellings stit, sis
origin Latin
meaning stand
anchor word statue

root **therm**
origin Greek
meaning heat
anchor word thermometer

root **vac**
origin Latin
meaning empty
anchor word vacant

prefix **sym**
other spellings syn
origin Greek
meaning together *or* with
anchor word sympathy

root **tort**
origin Latin
meaning twist
anchor word contortionist

root **val**
origin Latin
meaning strong
anchor word valiant

root **tain**
other spellings ten
origin Latin
meaning contain *or* hold
anchor word contain

root **typ**
origin Greek
meaning strike *or* impression
anchor word typewriter

prefix **zo**
origin Greek
meaning animal
anchor word zoo